Short Line Junction

Photo by Al Rose

Short Line Junction

A Collection Of California-Nevada Railroads

by

Jack R. Wagner

REVISED EDITION—1971

VALLEY PUBLISHERS
Fresno, California

REVISED EDITION
by
VALLEY PUBLISHERS
1759 Fulton Street
Fresno, California
1971

PRINTED IN THE UNITED STATES OF AMERICA

To my
mother and father

FOREWORD

As a small boy in a small town it was my ambition to run a locomotive, on any railroad, long or short. Boys and girls in small towns and on farms in those days almost universally looked forward to the day they could get on a train and they were not concerned whether the Interstate Commerce Commission classified the railroad as I, II or III, or as more generally known—a system, a trunk line or a short line.

Succeeding crops of kids have in turn been intrigued by the automobile, the bus and, finally, by the airplane. There still remains, though, particularly with us older folks, a memory of our first love, which is not likely to die. Methods may change, but human nature never. For this reason, if no other, there is much enjoyment packed between the covers of this book.

Jack Wagner's collection of humorous and historical tales concerning a typical group of western short lines is authentic and complete. His technical approach to the subject combines the methods of a historian with the genial good nature of a well-informed public relations man.

This is obviously not a book written in the back room of a public library. True, much of his information did come from old books, files and company records, but much more came from personal contact with railroad officials and railroaders alike. Some of the incidents told here were related across the desks of executive offices, while others were told over a tin cup of caboose coffee, or hollered across the cab of a swaying locomotive.

Jack Wagner's appearance with camera and work clothes will be remembered by many a short line railroader and because of his efforts the dramatic stories of these western short lines are made readily accessible for the entertainment and instruction of this and of all generations to come.

J. M. Hood, *President*
The American Short Line Railroad Association

Washington, D. C.

INTRODUCTION

There are throughout the United States a number of little railroads called short lines. These carriers, ranging from a mile or two in length to several hundred in some cases, were usually built for the purpose of bringing rail transportation to some isolated community or industry or perhaps a prosperous but lonely agricultural district.

The future of these short lines is an unknown factor. With increasing truck and bus competition each year finds the little railroads confronted with a tougher "row to hoe" and consequently each year sees one or more drop from sight. There is no doubt that before this book is very old the wheel of fortune will most surely spell death for some unlucky short line and the grim reaper in the form of the junk man will carry away the remains.

However, in spite of difficulties many of the short lines still operate and remain a solid American institution. For this reason I wish to avoid giving the impression that we are dealing with a "haywire" system of transportation or planting the frustrating seeds of a lost cause. Many of these railroads will be in service as long as a flanged wheel turns on a steel rail. Today, much of this country's lumber, ore and farm produce begins its journey to market over the picturesque route of a short line railroad and many a little road has chalked up revenues that are the envy of its bigger brothers.

But good times or bad the short line will always remain tops in human interest and sentimental appeal, and

to many a small town youth a veteran short line locomotive with clanking side rods and leaking steam chests
has been his first contact with the wonders of the outside
world. And if you have ever lived in a community far
beyond the ports of call of the fast freights and colorful
streamliners then you too will agree with the slogan,
originated by the Bath & Hamondsport, that "A Short
Line is a Hell-of-a-lot better than no line."

The above paragraphs were written in 1956 when
SHORT LINE JUNCTION first appeared. Since that time a
lot has happened to the railroad industry in the United
States. Passenger service has all but disappeared, railroad
lines have been allowed to merge in order to put up a more
solid economic front, a move that failed to forestall
bankruptcy in the historic Penn-Central case.

But, in spite of heavy operating costs, excessive
regulation and a host of other problems the railroad still
remains one of the most efficient methods for the move-
ment of large quantities of goods and material and through
it all the short line still lives.

The statement that I made in 1956 that much of this
country's lumber, ore and bulk produce begins its journey
to market over the picturesque route of a short line
railroad remains as true today as then. I am further pleased
to note that six of my favorite short lines (California
Western, Yreka Western, McCloud River RR, Quincy RR,
Sierra RR and the Nevada Northern) have all escaped the
junk man and are making their regular runs out to the
"junction." The California Western, in fact, is probably the
only common carrier railroad in the country today show-
ing a profit on its passenger service.

So you can see the end of the "short line story" has
not yet been told. For this reason I have not attempted to
completely rewrite SHORT LINE JUNCTION and the

publisher has elected to reissue by popular demand what has become a standard work in its field. Because SHORT LINE JUNCTION deals with the beginning, the who, what, where and why of seven short line railroads in California and Nevada, the research and historical material contained remains undated.

There have been changes, of course, in personnel and equipment and although I have not attempted to record the former I have in the "Appendix Update" listed equipment roster changes and other information of interest to the serious railfan accurate to the best of my ability.

I find words are a poor medium with which to thank the many people who assisted in the preparation of this book. To be sure much help and encouragement came from friends of long standing, but a great deal also came from people who were up to this time total strangers. These new friends, who range from the presidents and general managers down to the section hands, have contributed the history, anecdotes and human interest stories that go with life on a short line. Knowing them was to me the discovery of a friendly class of people who liked their work and enjoyed talking about it. My only hope is that they will enjoy seeing their little railroads in print as much as I have enjoyed writing about them.

Special mention should go to my good friends Roy D. Graves of San Francisco, for supplying many of the photographs; Curtis Ingram, who took time out to accompany me on many of my short line adventures; the late Graham Hardy, collector and dealer in Railroadiana, for photographs; Ted Wurm, railroad writer and historian of Oakland, for photographs and editorial assistance; D. S. Richter, motive power authority for supplying missing information; R. A. Regalia, assistant general manager of the California Western Railroad for information on that railroad and to Cathy Furniss for photographs; Lynn T.

Cecil, vice president and general manager of the Yreka Western; Guido Cottini, vice president McCloud River Railroad; Orval A. Myers, general superintendent Quincy Railroad Company; F. R. Egan, vice president and general manager Sierra Railroad Company; H. M. Peterson, vice president and general superintendent Nevada Northern Railway Company; Francis A. Guido, editor and publisher of the Western Railroader and Mike Pechner of radio station KCBS. My thanks, also, to the California Public Utilities Commission; the staff of the Hopkins Transportation Library, Stanford University; the staff of the Bancroft Library of the University of California, Berkeley; and to the many others who through interest and cooperation made this book possible.

Jack Russell Wagner

January, 1971
Sausalito, California

TABLE OF CONTENTS

Motor car No. 80 crosses the Noyo River on one of the modern steel bridges that replaced the old "A" Frame structures.

CHAPTER I
THE REDWOOD ROUTE

ED HENDRICKSON, RETIRED LOCOMOTIVE ENGINEER (now almost 90 and still living in Fort Bragg,) opened a box containing old photographs, picture post cards and personal effects. "Here's what the newspaper said about the day we took the first train over," Ed explained as he handed over the clipping. It read:

"Fort Bragg (Calif.) had a great day on Tuesday, December 19, 1911, the greatest day in her history and perhaps the greatest day to come—at least for some time. It was a great day in the broadest sense of the word, and those in that party—we venture—will always refer to it as one of the most happy moments of their lives, when the coast of Mendocino County was bound with steel rails, on one of the grandest and most scenic routes in the State of California, with the interior, giving direct communication with the outside world."

That's what some now forgotten country journalist had to say when the first train cautiously made its way over the forty mile California Western Railroad between Fort Bragg located on California's rugged north coast and the picturesque mountain community of Willits.

The newspaper account continues with a flourish to describe the trip over the mountains and the arrival in Willits to the accompaniment of blowing whistles and ringing bells plus the enthusiastic tooting of a brass band. And from what we can learn today the celebrations which followed at the Hotel Willits and later at the Hotel Windsor at Fort Bragg were something to behold. It's quite doubtful that as much noise was made when the Central Pacific met the Union Pacific and joined the entire continent. But before you snicker at the fuss made over the opening of a forty mile short line, consider for a moment what this project meant to the communities involved.

As late as 1911 Fort Bragg, a small town of about 2500, was effectively isolated from the rest of the state by a range of mountains on one side and the ocean on the other. In that day mountain roads were better suited to oxen than the feeble automobiles of the time, making the isolation formidable indeed. The best, if not the only, method of transportation was supplied by the little coastal steamers that braved the rocky coast line of Northern California to service the small seaside towns.

To the Fort Braggers, then, the new railroad meant an end to their isolation. Since Willits was on the main line of the Northwestern Pacific, it was now possible to reach San Francisco by rail.

The people of Willits were celebrating also. Perhaps some were rejoicing sympathetically with the delegation from Fort Bragg. No doubt others were merely celebrating something to celebrate, but the serious minded business man of Willits was celebrating the fact that his city was now a "two railroad town". "Yes, sir," you might have overheard a local booster exclaim, "Willits is the division point on the Northwestern Pacific and the eastern terminal of the California Western. She'll grow now—you just watch."

Well, Willits did grow—a little. It never did become the "Chicago of the West" as some of the more enthusiastic local boys would have had you believe that day, but it still is an important stop on the Northwestern Pacific, as well as California's famous Redwood Highway and it still is the eastern terminus of the California Western; so you might say it's holding its own.

Since railroads aren't built just to connect two communities, however isolated they might be, let's talk with the old timers, dig out the yellowing books and records and piece together the story that led up to the day of the first train.

In fact let's go all the way back to the year 1852 when a ship in the fabulous Oriental trade was driven off her course and missing the Golden Gate by some 150 miles wrecked herself on the Mendocino Coast. The crew took to the boats, rowing the entire distance to San Francisco. Once injected into the life stream of that city it didn't take long for the story of the rich cargo of silk to leak out.

Immediately salvage parties left for the scene of the wreck, but whether or not they ever found the ship is not recorded. They did, however, bring back tales of the vast stand of redwoods that covered the north coast for countless miles.

Among those who listened intently to the returning treasure seekers was one Harry Meiggs, local promoter and operator of Meiggs' Wharf. Stirred by these descriptions, Meiggs bought some mill machinery, loaded it on the ship "Ontario" and set out for the forests. Landing in a cove in the vicinity of Big River, which isn't very big as rivers go, Meiggs and his crew set up the mill and began operations as The California Lumber Company.

Impressed with the success of this project Captain William A. Richardson, a wealthy San Franciscan and the holder of large land grants in Mendocino, built a water-powered mill at Albion, a little south of Meiggs' location, and another at Noyo where the silk ship was reported to have grounded.

The local natives, who were natives indeed, being Indians under the leadership of Chief Noyo, resented the encroachment upon their hunting and fishing grounds proceeded to make it hot for the early lumbermen. This they accomplished by means of periodic raids which finally ended in the burning of the mill at Noyo.

In 1857 the United States Army was sent into the region to quell the Indian uprisings. The troops established headquarters about a mile north of Noyo and they called the settlement Fort Bragg. With the Indian menace out of the way the logging operations began to expand and prosper and the combined output of the mills kept the little lumber schooners constantly on the run.

It was about 1885 when C. R. Johnson came to the Pacific Coast from Michigan to purchase an interest in the Stewart & Hunter Lumber Company which was then working in the country north of Fort Bragg. Later the company expanded its operations to include the timberland around Fort Bragg and made that community the site of its big mill.

Johnson's outfit, which developed into the huge Union Lumber Company, operated its own steamship line to deliver their product to San Francisco and ports south. Employed on the line were skippers with colorful handles such as "Midnight" Olsen; so called because he could put his ship in a Mendocino dog-hole, as the tiny inlets were called, in the blackest midnight.

As the logging operations continued the timber naturally receded, widening the distance between the camps and the mill until the problem of transporting the logs from the woods to the sawyers was no longer a small one.

At first huge teams of oxen were used, but finally steel rails proved superior and from then on it was not unusual to see the steam schooners arrriving with locomotives, rails and other supplies necessary to build a railroad.

Combination car purchased from the L. A. Terminal railroad being loaded aboard coastal steamer in San Francisco bound for Fort Bragg. (About 1909)

Locomotive No. 5 arrives at Fort Bragg aboard the "National City",
an early coastal steamer built by Hay & Wright of San Francisco
in 1888 and sold to Peru in 1918.

J. E. French

No. 5 at work hauling lumber and logs on the C. W. about 1910.
In photo Will Langley, Dave Coon and Jim Gordon. Fred Hanson
on gangway. (No. 5 turned over with engineer Ed Hendrickson.
Cause wet weather and undercut track.)

J. E. French

Before the completion of the railroad, there was a stage connection from Willits to end o' track where passengers changed to the train.

No. 8 on a California Western passenger run in 1912.
From left to right: Ed Hendrickson, engineer; John Primental; Tom Wiley; Art Hanson (Fred Hanson's brother); In cab, Pat Dempsey. Others in picture are passengers.

Logging operations along the Noyo River. Note "A" frame bridge.

Photo: Randolph Brandt

Log dump at Pudding Creek on the California Western.

J. E. French

At first huge teams of oxen were used, but finally steel rails proved superior and from then on it was not unusual to see the steam schooners arriving with locomotives, rails and other supplies necessary to build a railroad.

As the redwood giants fell the timber frontier moved farther into the mountains taking with it the new railroad. At first "end o' track" was Hay Shed then South Fork and Ranch. This last stop was the company ranch where beef and hogs were raised, fruits and vegetables grown for the savory cook house meals that kept many a lumber jack in the woods.

On up the Noyo canyon the rails went, next to Redwood Lodge where a shingle mill was starting up, then to Grove, Camp 3 and Camp 4. The trees were huge now and when the rail gang came to a stump ten or more feet across they didn't remove it—they just built around it. Finally the little community of Alpine, eighteen miles from Fort Bragg, was reached. Here the road rested long enough for Alpine to become quite a little mountain village. The main attraction was Duffy's Mill which was considered a large operation for that day. There was also an early day resort called the Alpine Tavern which attracted many tourists to the area. There was a stage connection from Willits which brought visitors into the hostelry and also any passengers who wanted to transfer to the railroad at Alpine for the trip into Fort Bragg. These early stages ran through the Sherwood Valley into Willits and were operated by Leonard Barnard, who later became a banker and leading citizen of Fort Bragg.

The trip in by stage was something of an experience, especially when horseless carriages made the run. It was not at all unusual to see the passengers out on the road lending a shoulder to the wheel. Even when the auto did operate under its own power the going was far from smooth. If the traveler to Fort Bragg by this route was looking forward to leaving the lurching auto at Alpine for the luxury of rail travel he was doomed to disappointment, because in place of the red plush seats he might have expected, he found himself occupying one of the wooden benches built on a flat car and the rest of the journey was behind a creaking log train.

In the years that followed, the railroad was extended to Camp 6, Camp 7 and North Spur. The Alpine outfit moved up to the new railhead leaving the little community without visible means of support. A forest fire destroyed the hotel and the few remaining buildings. Today all that remains of Alpine is the little railway station with a sign that records the name of a once busy town.

The tracks next ran through the timber holdings of the Irvine & Muir Lumber Company, stopping only long enough to build a station which was named "Irmulco", using the first letters from each word in the company's title. On the rails went, passing or establishing new communities as they advanced. At Soda Springs a new stage connection was made. This time the ride from Willits to the railroad was much shorter although just as rough.

So it was, the railroad that started out to follow the loggers found itself so close to the summit of the mountains, which had once been considered a barrier, that the company became aware of the feasibility of building down the other side and into Willits.

The surveyors and engineers reported that most of the bridges and trestles were behind them and with the exception of one tunnel at the summit the rest of the road would be comparatively simple. It was decided, then, to continue construction . . . and so the little railroad that started out with nothing particular in mind ended up at Willits in 1911.

Regarding the first train the newspaper article continues:

"It was a quarter past nine o'clock on the morning of December 19, 1911 when Superintendent J. C. French, of the California Western Railroad and Navigation Company, opened the throttle of locomotive No. 5, with three cars attached, ably assisted by Ed Hendrickson (engineer) and Conductor Fred Hanson, pulled out of Fort Bragg depot, with a little less than one hundred and fifty people, to greet the people of Willits, with the first train (complimentary excursion) passing over the road to Willits. It was a jolly crowd, all bent on a good time, which they had. Superintendent F. C. White of the Union Lumber Company, did everything possible to make all feel at home, and succeeded admirably. The trip along the beautiful Noyo River is always enjoyable, but on this occasion it was doubly so, all realizing the importance of the event, everything passing off splendid."

Mr. French, who was then superintendent of the road, handled the throttle most of the way over and back. According to his daughter, Miss Vera French now living in Santa Clara, California, the road was not completely ballasted at the time of the first train and French didn't feel that such great responsibility should rest on any employe. Miss French says that she well recalls how after the return trip her father went right to bed with a sick headache, thereby missing the Fort Bragg celebration at the Hotel Windsor and the dance that followed in the Red Men's Hall.

Because of the unfinished condition of the roadbed and a tunnel fire that burned for months the railroad didn't officially begin service until July 4, 1912.

Today a ride on the California Western is as exciting and picturesque as it was the day it opened. True the steam locomotives are gone and all of the passenger and express traffic is now carried by skunks (rail motor cars) but the ride through the redwoods, over the 1,740 foot summit and along the Noyo River canyon is still one of thrills.

Starting out from Willits early in the morning on one of the two a day motor cars you immediately begin the 3.3% grade to Summit. Passing through tunnel No. 2 at the top of the divide you then begin the 3% drop into Fort Bragg. During this thirty-five mile piece of twisting track gravity supplies the motive power making frequent air applications necessary to hold down the speed, while at the same time a special attachment at the front of the car sprays water on the rails to act as a lubricant for the sharp curves.

When the road opened it listed two tunnels and 115 bridges in forty miles of right-of-way. Today the two tunnels remain, but the engineering department has pared down the number of bridges and trestles to forty-four. Nine of the remaining bridges are the old "A" frame type trusses, but these are being replaced by more modern construction.

The ride from Willits to Fort Bragg graphically demonstrates how the mountain residents depend on the friendly little railway. It's an every day occurrence to see a rolled newspaper flung from the cab to the pathway of some isolated subscriber. As for stops between terminals, they might be a Boy Scout camp (Camp Silverado, the only Boy Scout camp in the country that has no road into it) or a fisherman's tent, it doesn't really matter. If there's a box of groceries to be delivered or a service to be rendered then that's reason enough.

To many people along the line the railroad represents the only communication with the outside world even to this day. Take the time the stork ventured way out on that mountain line far from highway competition. A frantic telephone call brought engineer John Galliani and conductor Joe Silva out into the night on the first available conveyance they could find—the section foreman's speeder. The two men wrapped the expectant mother in blankets and began a historic race. There were no opposing trains so it was full speed all the way. Perhaps the little car should have displayed green marker lights on the head end, because behind them streaked a phantom second section with Death at the throttle. But John Galliani proved himself to be the better runner and a hasty Caesarean at the Willits Hospital saved two lives before the grim reaper pulled into town.

The California Western isn't a boomer's road. Most of the hands are old timers with "whiskers" a yard long. Take Fred Hanson, for instance, who first went to work for the company in 1905. He was the conductor on the first train over the hill and eventually became superintendent of transportation, a position he held until his retirement. Fred's nephew, Louis Hanson, is now a conductor, the second generation of Hansons to work for the California Western.

Then there's Claude King. Before World War I he worked on the old Northern Electric, but when he came back from being a soldier he found that the road had been sold and was now a part of the Sacramento Northern. His job wasn't waiting for him. Following a hunch he set out for the lumber country. Arriving in Fort Bragg with only $1.75 in his jeans, he made a connection that kept him happy and well fed for most of his working life. At the time I knew Claude King he was chief dispatcher, however he has since retired from railroad service and is living at Fort Bragg still grateful for that urge to go north that came to him 36 years ago.

It was much the same with Russel Todd, the roundhouse foreman, also retired by now. He kept 'em running for the California Western for over 25 years. He liked the work and the country, a happy combination that kept him on the job.

The record, though, is probably held by Ed Hendrickson. When Ed retired from service as an engineer he had chalked up forty years of mountain railroading. He estimates that during that time he had hauled enough logs to reach around the world some three and one half times!

Railroading on a logging road isn't all duck soup. This type of road is known to take its share of life and limb, but the boys can always find time to have a good laugh or spin a yarn. Claude King's favorite story, for instance, deals with a circus train they were pulling over the mountain. One of the gayly painted cars was a long, underslung "possum belly" that barely cleared on some of the curves. Finally there came an extra sharp one that caused the side of the car to scrape the bank, splitting it open as it rubbed. When the train arrived at Fort Bragg it was discovered that the occupants of the car—monkeys, had seized the opportunity to resign from show business and had fled to the trees. For several seasons reports came back from people who were startled to see monkeys scampering through the redwoods. Had it not been for an extra hard winter, cold enough to severely damage even their brass counterparts, there might still be a band of redwood primates swinging through the Mendocino hills.

Engineer John Galliani, now the old timer on the road, tells one on himself. He had met the Northwestern Pacific train from San Francisco at Willits and was heading motor car No. 100 over the rails toward Fort Bragg. On this car the engineer's box is in the forward end of the baggage section. John had ridden with some strange loads during his years with the railroad, but this dark night he was hauling something he had never hauled before. It was a pine box transferred from the NWP and consigned to Fort Bragg— a box containing a corpse! Now John isn't exactly a nervous man, but as the trees danced in the yellow beam of the swaying headlight his imagination began to play strange tricks. Suddenly as the car plunged into the complete blackness of tunnel Number 2 there came from the baggage section a low moan. The engineer risked a quick glance over his shoulder, but everything seemed in order. No sooner had his eye settled on the rails ahead, however, he heard it again . . . a low gutteral cry that seemed to come from that oblong box. By the time he pulled into the Fort Bragg station John was beginning to doubt his sanity, but he was no coward. He even helped unload his cargo. Finally when the pile of packages and boxes was thinning down he found the clue that solved the case of the groaning corpse. It was a crate containing a small pig!

Fred Hanson likes to recall the days prior to 1930 when the railroad ran full sized passenger trains with Pullman service that connected with the Northwestern Pacific making Fort Bragg a pleasant overnight trip from the City. A few miles out of Fort Bragg the incoming varnish would stop at a company cook house and pick up a supply of coffee and donuts which would be served to the morning passengers with the "compliments of the California Western Railroad & Navigation Company". This, of course, was before the days of the skunks, as the bright yellow motor cars are affectionately known for miles around.

All the freight runs are at night, when the skunks are in the car house and their crews asleep. Twenty cars is the usual consist for the road's two Baldwin Diesel Locomotives. "Sometimes," says A. T. Nelson, vice president and general manager of the road, "the train will take 30 cars—and that means 3 trips over the summit." Either of the Diesels would handle 30 to 40 heavily loaded cars on level track, but on the climb to the summit 10 loads are about all the two combined can handle, according to Nelson.

In spite of the fact Pullman service and free coffee and donuts are only memories, time hasn't done too badly by the California Western. In fact now that the picturesque steam schooners have disappeared from coastal shipping the California Western now carries the entire output of the mills at Fort Bragg and when the nightly thunder of tandum Diesels echoes up and down the Noyo canyon local residents know that another train load of lumber is finding its way to the markets of the world.

Tomorrow's skunk will bring the City papers and the mail.

No. 5 again. This time as an oil burner. On ground, H. P. Plummer
who later became sales manager for the Union Lumber Company.
At extreme right, Otis Johnson son of the Mill's founder C. R. Johnson.

J. E. French

Early "A" Frame bridge over the Noyo River. Today the engineering department has pared down the number of bridges and trestles
to forty-four. Nine of the remaining bridgs are the old "A" Frame
type trusses, but these are being replaced by more modern construction.

J. E. French

J. E. French

Locomotive No. 4 of the California Western Railroad & Navigation Company as a wood burner around 1901.

Lower photo taken on a passenger run after her conversion to oil.

Randolph Brandt

Dumping logs at the Union Lumber Company's mill at Fort Bragg.

British Bark Yeoman Loading lumber by cable at Noyo Harbor. The Yeoman was sunk during World War I by the German Raider Sea-adler commanded by Count Von Luckner.

Randolph Brandt

No. 8 and a load of big ones. After she was scrapped, engineer Ed Hendrickson claimed he heard her whistle on a San Francisco Bay ferry. This could have been checked because No. 8's whistle had the date 1881 stamped across the top.

Randolph Brandt

Union Lumber Company mill at Fort Bragg after the 1906 earthquake.

J. E. French

The "Yolo". Locomotive No. 3 on the California Pacific running from Benicia to Sacramento before the completion of the transcontinental railroad. She came to California via Cape Horn. The California Western bought her and renumbered her No. 6. Her last days were spent on the Redwood Route.

Built by Baldwin in 1901, this 0-6-0 originally worked for the Arizona & New Mexico then became the El Paso & Southwest's No. 30. This photo was taken the day she arrived at Fort Bragg to become the California Western No. 41. Scrapped by C. W. in 1936.

California Western No. 38 before she was scrapped in 1941. Formerly the "Malone" (#39) of the Central Pacific of California she became Southern Pacific 1529 and 2002. When the California Western first acquired her, she was their #8, but somehow or other she worked herself up to #38.

Typical California Western Caboose. Color: Yellow.

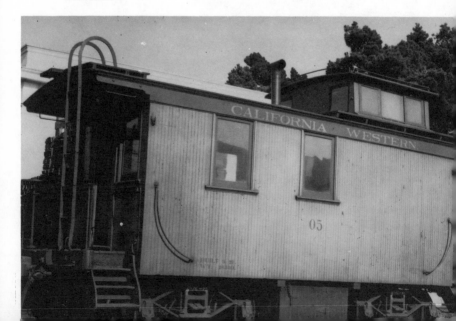

ourist folder
sued by the
alifornia Western R. R.
1917.

No. 23. Typical of the well-maintained motive power of the California Western Railroad. Built by Baldwin in 1923 - Scrapped 1950.

Wonacott's Studio

California Western No. 21 pulling into Fort Bragg with a train load of logs from the "Ten Mile" branch. July 1, 1940.

TECRASILK PHOTO

No. 80. The first "skunk" to appear on the C. W. Built by the Mack Motor Car Company in 1925.

D. S. Richter

Going west (downhill) between Crater and Clare Mill the train enters a reverse curve on a fill. This was formerly an "S" shaped trestle but was filled.

TECRASILK PHOTO

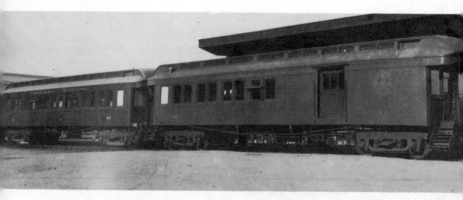

Coaches 42 and 43, passenger equipment of a bygone day.

TECRASILK PHOTO

Formerly a 7th Street local in Oakland this coach found its way to the C. W. to become No. 44.

Photo, Roy D. Graves

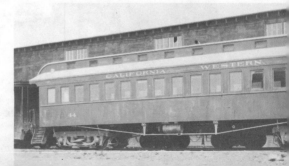

No. 12 was a Baldwin tank locomotive. Built in 1915 and scrapped in 1950.

Photo by Roy D. Graves

o. 11 at "Ten Mile"
5 miles north of Fort
agg) May 1937. She
as a Baldwin built in
913 and scrapped in
47.

to by Roy D. Graves

No. 14. Built in 1924 by Baldwin she was retained for standby use. The only steam locomotive now on the California Western.

Photo by A. T. Nelson

Diesel motor car M 100, one of three "skunks" that provide passenger, mail and express service on the California Western.

Photo by John P. Carrick

Trona Railway motor car No. 22 as it appeared on that road before being purchased by the California Western.

Photo from Randolph Brandt

With new lettering and paint job Trona Railway #22 now rolls along the Noyo River Canyon as California Western M 200.

Photo by Curtis Ingram

California Western Railroad & Navigation Co.
TRAIN SCHEDULE

MOTOR COACH		STATIONS	MOTOR COACH	
3 DAILY	1 DAILY		2 DAILY	4 DAILY
5:00 PM	10:00 AM	Lv Fort Bragg Ar	4:00 PM	9:00 AM
5:17	10:17	South Fork	3:41	8:41
5:24	10:24	Ranch	3:35	8:35
5:28	10:28	Redwood Lodge	3:30	8:30
5:33	10:33	Grove	3:24	8:24
5:43	10:43	Camp Silverado	3:14	8:14
5:47	10:47	Alpine	3:09	8:09
5:51	10:51	Camp Marwedel	3:05	8:05
5:52	10:52	Olde Camp Seven	3:04	8:04
5:55	10:55	Northspur	3:00	8:00
6:05	11:05	Irmulco	2:50	7:50
6:11	11:11	Shake City	2:44	7:43
6:27	11:27	Clare Mill	2:34	7:32
6:38	11:38	Crowley	2:27	7:24
6:50	11:50	Summit	2:19	7:15
7:00 PM	12:01 PM	Ar Willits Lv	2:05 PM	7:00 AM

NOTE: Camp supplies, provisions and small parcels will be handled in Motor Car Service at Tariff Rates.

A. T. NELSON, *General Manager*
FORT BRAGG, CALIFORNIA

Numbers 21 and 22 and little No. 1 display a generation of California Western motive power in a photo taken in the days when steam was king.

Photo by Wonacott's Studio

Steam still lives on the California Western with the acquisition of #45, a Baldwin 2-8-2 in 1965 and more recently #46, a Baldwin Mallet (above). Purchased in April 1969 from Rayonier, Inc. in Hoquiam, Washington where it operated as a saddle tank it was brought to Fort Bragg for a complete overhaul.

(California Western Railroad)

No. 46 after her complete renovation at the California Western shops. Placed in service August 24, 1970 the #46 now joins #45 in heading the popular "Super Skunk" the only regularly scheduled standard gauge steam passenger train in California if not the country still operated by a common carrier railroad.

(California Western Railroad)

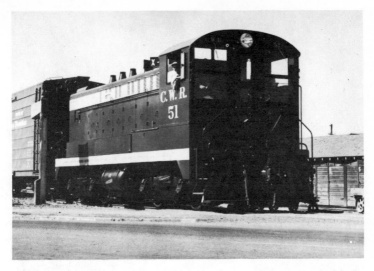

Today the road's freight motive power consists of two Baldwin 750 h.p. Diesels.

Steam power and four all-steel ex-Erie-Lackawanna coaches make up the increasingly popular "Super Skunk." This photo taken at Willits shows No. 45 at the headend.

CHAPTER II

SISKIYOU SHORT LINE

As on many other short lines, the engine crew of the Yreka Western doubles in brass; so even though there wasn't a train due to leave until late that night it wasn't unusual to find engineer Harold Thomas and his fireman, George Calkins, puttering around the round house at three in the afternoon.

Thomas stopped cranking the blower of the forge long enough to remove his glove and shake hands. His manner was quiet and not at all unfriendly. Calkins was fussing around in the cab of number eight so we climbed aboard to talk with him.

George Calkins, it turned out, was the old timer on the road. He had seen equipment, general managers and owners come and go, but through good times and bad George had remained philosophically a fireman of locomotives. When he was a young man, George took a job digging a mine shaft. It paid better than most jobs at the time (about $2 a day), but George wasn't satisfied. "One of these days," he reasoned, "this shaft will be down as far as they want it to go. Then what?" No, there wasn't any future in digging a hole in the ground. Someone had said that they needed a man over at the Yreka Railroad; so that's where he went. The pay wasn't nearly as good as his previous job, but the chances were good that the railroad would be running long after the miners had hit bottom.

In his new connection Calkins did fill his need for a steady job, but if he secretly had hoped to find the work easier he was doomed to disappointment. Those were the days of wood burning locomotives and the fireman not only pitched the cord wood into the firebox, he also loaded the tender at every fuel stop and sometimes even found it necessary to cut his own. During the dry season he frequently added another meaning to the title "fireman" as he attempted to extinguish the conflagrations started by the sparks from his locomotive.

George Calkins poured some oil on a bundle of waste, looked at it thoughtfully for a moment, then touching a match to the wad he suddenly tossed it through the fire door of the locomotive. Immediately there was a dull explosion and almost at once the firebox became a roaring inferno. Raising his voice as he adjusted the oil feed, he announced without dramatics, that he once fired a locomotive on bacon grease. And so as we sat on the sand box absorbing the warmth of the fire we heard the amazing story of the locomotive that ran on bacon grease.

During the wood burning days of the Yreka Railroad, it seems, one of the local merchants received a shipment of hams and bacons that spoiled. One day while the locomotive was on a siding near the unuseable shipment, the owner, anxious to get it out of his sight, asked Calkins if he wouldn't throw the cured pork on the tender and dump it in the river or some other place well out of town. So accommodating George Calkins loaded up with ham and bacon. Once they were under way engineer and fireman began to speculate on how best to get rid of their cargo. Finally, in an experimental mood, Calkins tossed a side of bacon into the fire. It went up like gun powder giving off an intense heat a thousand times better than any stick of wood they had on board. Immediately this spoilage took on added significance and was carefully placed in a corner of the tender. Thereafter whenever the little locomotive needed extra power a huge plume of black smoke could be seen coming from the diamond stack and for some time after the train disappeared over the hill there mysteriously lingered an aroma of crisp bacon or juicy baked ham.

The little city of Yreka, California is the headquarters and main excuse for the railroad. It is also the county seat of Siskiyou County and as such is the hub around which turns the governmental, social and economic life of a rich inland empire. The county itself contains a great variety of topography, climate and natural resources in its 6,256 square miles and is located in north central California bordering the state of Oregon and lying between 41 and 42 degrees north latitude. Its size is larger than the states of Connecticut and Rhode Island combined and its general appearance is that of a mountainous region generously supplied with wide fertile valleys.

The first white men to enter the region which is now Siskiyou County were trappers from the Hudson's Bay Company at Vancouver. Alexander McLeod in 1827, Jedediah Smith 1829, and Stephen Hall Meek in 1835, being among the first noted. In March of 1851, when the entire state was in the midst of gold fever, two prospectors named Thompson and Bell working their way north, discovered the precious metal on Yreka Flat. The site became known as "Thompson's Dry Diggin's" and within six weeks some two thousand people had arrived to see for themselves. Eventually a local government was formed and an alcalde named.

By the spring of 1852 the region had sufficient representation at the state capitol that a bill was introduced in the legislature to create the County of Siskiyou and change the name of the town to Yreka. Yreka it was and five years later it became an incorporated city.

To the visitor Yreka seems charmingly situated in the heart of the mountains, but to the more practical local businessman this picturesque location was seen as one reason the Southern Pacific preferred not to get any closer than six miles. This lack of direct rail transportation was definitely felt in the economy of the community. Finally when it appeared that things would not get any better until something was done, a group of local citizens decided to take the situation in hand. A railroad from Yreka to connect with the S.P. at Montague was proposed as a community enterprise and according to the original charter, still hanging in the Company office at Yreka, things officially got under way May 28, 1888.

There doesn't seem to be much information available on the actual construction of the road, but we can assume that it wasn't a very dramatic story. A fairly easy grade was found east of Yreka (maximum 2.3%), no tunnels were needed and only occasionally did a small trestle appear necessary (six times in fact), the largest one being across the Shasta River.

Outside of the fact that the first locomotives used were wood burners, perhaps the greatest contrast between early and present day operation lies in the road's source of revenue. According to Company records, 67% of the earnings came from passenger business during the early years of operation. In 1947 what few passengers were carried traveled by Company operated bus and contributed less than 1% of the total revenue. Today passenger service has been discontinued and the road operates for freight and express service only.

Unfortunately like so many well meaning community projects of this type, the little railroad was not exactly a profitable proposition, but it did manage to keep rolling for sixteen years or so under local management. At the end of that period, according to an entry in the books for June 6, 1904, one Joseph Johnson got the idea of extending the railroad into Scott Valley, a rich farming area one mountain range west of Yreka. Mr. Johnson may have had something there, although it would have been a costly project. At any rate, nothing ever came of the Scott Valley extension.

Late in 1905, however, the firm of Scott and Van Arsdell began dickering for the purchase of the railroad. They also announced their intention to extend the rails into Scott Valley and even to the community of Etna. Finally in April, 1906, the deal was completed and the Yreka Railroad was purchased by the new company. (The similarity of names between Scott, one of the new owners and Scott Valley is coincidental.)

On April 7, 1906, at a meeting of the board of directors of the Yreka Railroad Company, the new owners took over the property. The board members of the old company resigned one at a time and for each vacancy a new director was voted in thereby keeping a quorum at all times.

When the directorate was composed entirely of Scott and Van Arsdell men, election of officers was held with Mr. G. W. Scott emerging as the new president. (Mr. Scott was the Scott of Hall-Scott marine engine fame.) The future of the Yreka Railroad looked bright indeed . . . what with the new capital, new owners and plenty of enthusiasm. All of these factors pointed toward the final fulfillment of the Scott Valley Extension and other improvements.

But the optimism of local residents and new directors alike lasted for just eleven days! Fate was determined to have the last word and on the morning of April 18, 1906 the San Francisco earthquake and fire smashed all hope for the Yreka Railroad. Not that extensive damage was caused as far north as Siskiyou County, but to be sure the financial effects were. Mr. Scott and his associates were hard hit by the San Francisco disaster and the eagerness to invest additional money at this time was badly shaken. The plans to expand the operation were immediately cancelled and the railroad was left to operate as best it could.

Things weren't so good in the years that followed. The population of Yreka remained just about the same as it was when two thousand gold seekers arrived over fifty-five years before. Then, as the years wore on and the automobile had acquired enough horse power to negotiate even the roads of Siskiyou County, conditions grew still worse for the little railroad. This was the beginning of the gasoline era and the shadow of things to come had fallen on rusting rails. The automobile had been accepted as a practical means of transportation and was beginning to make inroads into all rail business. The Yreka Railroad, in its weakened condition, was in no position to enter a fight that would later see many a larger carrier hanging on the ropes.

In a last ditch effort to fight fire with fire the Scott company introduced, what was to become accepted procedure for practically all small railroads desiring to slash operating costs . . . the gasoline propelled combination passenger and baggage coach. One of the first of such cars and the *very* first one the Yreka railroaders had ever heard of was delivered to the Yreka Railroad. This early "skunk" was typical in appearance of all to come and was powered by a sixty horse power (undoubtedly a Hall-Scott) gasoline engine. But, even these economy measures proved to be of little help; so at length the Scott & Van Arsdell Company could hold out no longer and decided to give up.

But, the citizens of Yreka didn't want to see their city left without a railroad connection and so for the second time organized themselves for direct action. By popular subscrip-

Locomotive No. 1 of the Yreka Railroad. Sitting is Jack Frizell, fireman, and standing in the gangway is engineer Archie De Lamontonia (his son is said to be working for the S.P. at Klamath Falls, Oregon). Photo taken around 1890.

Yreka Western Railroad

Apparently the Shasta River bridge was a favorite photo stop on the Yreka Railroad. Here is a construction photo taken in 1888. Below the wood burning No. 1 poses at the same spot.

Ernest Brazil

Old roundhouse at Yreka, California, as it appeared in 1936 during the dark days of the Yreka Railroad. Building destroyed by fire in 1938.

Photo courtesy D. R. Terrett

Passenger coach once used on the Yreka Railroad. Photo taken at Yreka August, 1936.

Photo courtesy D. R. Terrett

Combination coach used on the Yreka Railroad. Photo taken August, 1936.

No. 7 and train near Montague.

tion enough money was raised to buy back their railroad and on April 6th, 1920 the Yreka Railroad Company again belonged to the people.

Although entirely subsidized by the local citizenry, the dying railroad managed to keep up steam for another eight years. Finally in June 1928 the property was sold to the Klamath River Holding Company of which Mr. H. A. De-Vaux was president.

Once again new owners made an announcement of great plans for the future and once again the eight mile short line took on new hope. But, once again an unkind fate held the trump card. The year was 1928!

How the years of depression were to affect the Yreka Railroad is a story in itself. The long years of curtailed traffic and greatly reduced revenue suffered by even the great systems of the country were all but fatal to the little road. All possible corners were cut and every conceivable expense was eliminated. Even the maintenance of the right-of-way was an extravagant luxury that the management could ill afford. As a result the ties, suffering from compound fractures, turned up at the ends and the spikes were so loose that frequently the weight of the locomotive would turn the rail completely over. The gauge varied by an unbelievable amount and when the rails were even with each other it was only when they passed each other going in opposite directions. A trip to the junction with the Southern Pacific at Montague was usually made more on the ground than on the rail and even when on the rail four miles an hour was considered top speed. Some-times the run ran into days and it's a safe guess that the Yreka Railroad in those trying times contained more grief per mile than any other road in the country.

But, in spite of everything the railroad continued to operate under the direction of Mr. DeVaux. DeVaux was typically and characteristically a promoter and of all things said about him, good and bad, it must truthfully be added that he saw the railroad through its darkest hour and regarding his administration, it will perhaps not be too libelous to say here that Mr. DeVaux kept the railroad operating by "hook or crook."

There seems to be litle doubt that DeVaux was somewhat of a "sharpie" with a flare for putting up a good front. As an insight into his methods and personality the people of Yreka still tell the story of his trip to Florida one winter.

It seems that while trying to forget the cares of the day at a fashionable beach resort Mr. DeVaux felt the need of a type of consolation that could be supplied only by the best and most expensive cigars. Promptly putting his desires into action he called on the most exclusive cigar manufacturer in town. Presenting his business card, which introduced him as H. A. DeVaux, president of the Yreka Railroad Company, he glibly made his proposition. With a little flattery here and there, he smoothly explained to the cigar maker that he was interested in obtaining the best cigars money could buy for the dining car service on his railroad. After a little pleasant conversation DeVaux left the store with a box each of the 50¢ and $1 variety under his arm as "samples". Had the cigar-maker consulted a copy of the "Railway Guide", he would have known that the Yreka Railroad offered very little service of any kind and certainly least of all dining car accommodations.

In August, 1933, the Yreka Railroad went through the throes of reorganization, after which it emerged as the Yreka Western Railroad. Apparently little was changed but the name as conditions failed to improve. Finally hitting a new low in 1935, the property was listed in a foreclosure action and judicial sale where it was purchased by Vince Delano and Carl W. Fawcett.

It was also about this time that a practice carried on during the long lean years came to a head. It appeared that the little railroad, which had seen so little cash, just couldn't bear to turn over to the Southern Pacific its share of the freight money collected at the Yreka end of the haul. The larger road brought suit against the short line in the Superior Court and was well on its way toward taking it out of its hide when the late A. D. Schader, a San Francisco railroad contractor, stepped in and purchased the Southern Pacific's claim. Schader then acquired the outstanding stock and became the sole owner of the Yreka Western.

O. G. Steele of Yreka, operated the road as receiver. His policy of making railroad property available to mills and other industries soon had its effect on business and before long the little terminal at Yreka was a beehive of activity. The new ownership began to rehabilitate the railroad by reinvesting some of the new earnings in roadbed and equipment.

Two steam locomotives, No. 7 and No. 8, were purchased from the State Belt Railroad in San Francisco. They remained the work horses of the road until 1954 when No. 19 was acquired from the McCloud River Railroad giving the Yreka Western a stable of three iron horses; all steam and all in good condition.

The receivership has been terminated for several years and the Yreka Western has been operating on a solid corporate basis with O. G. Steele remaining as vice-president and chief operating officer.

The railroad is now gravel ballasted and relaid with good 75 pound rail. It has been pronounced the best short line road bed in California.

As with many of the mountain railroads these days, lumbering and logging activity is responsible for much of the prosperity. Some of this, of course, is temporary, although the larger mills can be depended on for freight revenue for years to come. And fortunately there are other shippers who help pay the way with a variety of commodities. For instance, the county is rich in agriculture and business in general is healthy and active. Ever since the days of "Thompson's Dry Diggings" Siskiyou County has been a leading mineral producer.

Perhaps the most unusual of the regular loads to travel on the Yreka Western are the tank cars of the local gas comany. Without pipe line or local manufacturing plant, all of the community's heating gas is hauled up in special tank cars under pressure and released into the gas company's storage tank at Yreka.

So for the past ten years or so things have been looking up for the Yreka Western. As a matter of fact in 1954 the little road grossed $205,000.00 and even with a payroll of around $100,000 plus operating expenses it managed to show a $40,000 net.

But 1954 was also a sad year for the Yreka Western for in December Al Schader, its owner and chief benefactor, died. The presidency went to Herbert F. Baker of San Francisco, a long time friend and business associate of Schader.

Although Baker's career strangely paralleled that of Al Schader, it wasn't until 1924 that the two met in San Francisco. Upon comparing notes it was discovered that both men grew up in Ozark County, Missouri. Some time after leaving home Baker became chief clerk to the division superintendent for the Chicago, Milwaukee & St. Paul Railroad . . . at Three Forks, Montana. Baker was quite proud of his accomplishment as he was the youngest chief clerk on the system. But he didn't know that another poor boy from Missouri was at that same time making a name for himself on the next division as the road's youngest roadmaster. His name was Al Schader.

Herbert Baker enjoys being the president of a railroad even if he only gets $1 a year and a pass from Montague to

Yreka. The memory of his friend, Al Schader and his fondness for railroads in general makes the duties a pleasure. But, Baker has another job. As coexecutor of the Shader estate it will be his job to find a buyer for the eight mile railroad to satisfy the terms of the will.

So once again the Yreka Western must change hands, but this time it's a going concern supplying a necessary service to the community.

Fireman George Calkins and Engineer Harold Thomas (standing).

Photo by Curtis Ingram 1946

During the lean years the Yreka Railroad suffered many derailments due to the poor roadbed.

The big hook, courtesy of the Southern Pacific, has arrived to reclaim one of the SP's bashed in box cars.

With a good road bed and heavy rail the rebuilt Yreka Western is now virtually trouble free.

All photos courtesy
D. R. Terrett

Leaving Yreka the train climbs Butcher Hill as it heads east toward Montague.

Early morning in the Siskiyous. Stone building is an old powder house.

Photo by Jack R. Wagner 1947

An outgoing train.

The Shasta River bridge as it looks today.

Y. W. locomotive pulls into the S. P. station at Montague.

Photos by Jack R. Wagner

Outgoing logs are big revenue on the Yreka Western

Photo by Jack R. Wagner

In 1950 the Y. W. tried out a brand new Diesel.

On test run a lumber truck collided with locomotive at a highway crossing.

Truck driver was killed.

Photos by Jack R. Wagner

INTERCHANGE AT MONTAGUE

The Southern Pacific band comes to town to play at the County
Fair and is met by YW No. 8 and pulled into Yreka.

The YW turning over a trainload of logs to the SP. They will now
ride the SP Siskiyou Line to the Fruit Grower's Supply mill at Hilts.
Below: LCL freight for Scott's Valley goes by truck.

Photos by Jack R. Wagner

The home guard on the Yreka Western. Left to right: Engineer Harold Thomas, fireman George Calkins, conductor Al Glutsch, and brakeman Otis Tyrer.

No. 7 was formerly a city girl. She came from the State Belt Railroad in San Francisco, but ended her days on the Yreka Western in Siskiyou County. In this photo, taken in 1947, she waits patiently while her crew has breakfast at Montague.

CHAPTER III

EAST OF SHASTA

IN THE COUNTRY east of Mount Shasta in Northern California, where the population is thin and the timber thick, there operates one of the smoothest running short line railroads in the West. Taking its name from the snow-fed McCloud River, the McCloud River Railroad connects a vast timber area with three major railroads; the Southern Pacific, Great Northern and the Western Pacific.

The McCloud River Railroad's western terminus and junction with the Southern Pacific is Mt. Shasta City. Leaving the town of Mt. Shasta the rails head east running along the very base of the great snow covered mountain, the fourth highest peak in the United States.

At Signal Butte (MP 10.9), the road descends to the mill and company town of McCloud via one of the few remaining switchbacks to be found in modern railroading.

From McCloud the rails continue east to Hambone where the Great Northern has built a 34 mile branch in from its main line. McCloud River Railroad trains operate over this stretch, under a trackage agreement, to Lookout where interchange is made with the Great Northern and the Western

Pacific. Counting a brand new extension into Burney, which we will describe later, this gives the McCloud River Railroad about 130 miles of track to operate with some 98 miles directly owned by the company.

The town of McCloud is the headquarters for the railroad and here one finds the executive offices, shops, roundhouse, yards and all that goes to make up a busy railroad terminal. It is here that one gets the impression that the road is much larger than it actually is. This is probably due to the fact that everything is neat and businesslike with activity going on at every turn.

The building which houses the station and operating offices of the railroad is rustically built of native wood which lends architectural authenticity to the scene, although it does resemble a mountain lodge somewhat more than a railroad building. Inside, express men, freight clerks and ticket sellers go about their work while from somewhere in the building the muted ticking of a Morse sounder can be heard. Through a door lettered "train men only" we can see the dispatcher sitting before a switchboard. By an occasional call to points along the line he keeps his system operating smoothly and safely.

The McCloud River Railroad is a paradox and an optical illusion. It's large and yet it's small. You know full well that this is a short line, but the shops, yards and offices give it the appearance of a much larger road. You begin to feel that this was once one of the trunk lines that somehow or other has been compressed to fit into a miniature empire of its own. And when you look up and see the towering magnificence and brilliant whiteness of Mount Shasta, looking for all the world like an exaggerated backdrop, you begin to feel that the whole thing is unreal and somehow you have been reduced to Lilliputian proportions and the scene is the window of some department store and the time is Christmas. But this is only a passing thought. When a train of logs clatters past, you put aside all visions of toy trains and department store displays and return to the realities of the present. The scale in miles may be small, but the operation here is fast moving, efficient and plenty big time.

Climbing the stairs to the second floor of the headquarters building we find ourselves standing in the reception room presided over by an attractive young lady behind a desk. After being announced, we are ushered into the office of Mr. Flake Willis, president and general manager of the McCloud River Railroad Company.

The room is large, thickly carpeted and furnished in exceedingly good taste. We could be on Wall Street in New York or high above Montgomery Street down in San Francisco. It takes a quick glance outside to the ever present view of Mount Shasta to bring us back to McCloud. If, upon recovery, you are inclined to think it a little strange that such an attractive office should be so far off the beaten track you must remember you are calling on the president of the railroad and the executive offices of any railroad worth its salt should look the part.

Mr. Flake Willis, president of the McCloud River Railroad, talks railroading with ease and an air of authority that shows he is thoroughly familiar with the problems of other railroads in the country as well as his own. He speaks enthusiastically of the work of the American Short Line Railroad Association of which he is an active director.

Willis likes to tell how he began his railroading career in 1934 when at the age of 20 he was hired as station agent by the 72 mile Apache Railway in Arizona. Later he resigned to work for the A. T. & S. F. on the Albuquerque Division. He might still be with the Santa Fe if a personnel reduction hadn't forced him to seek back his old job of station agent with the Apache Railway. This time he stayed with the short line, eventually becoming traffic manager, general manager, vice-president and a director. In 1952 Flake Willis became president of the McCloud River Railroad. Yes, Willis knows railroading—every inch of it—right down from that mahogany desk at McCloud to the spikes in his new ties on the Burney extension.

Our next stop is Roadmaster F. C. Zeigler's office, but we are informed he is out on the road some place and won't be in until late. This we can understand as he is the man who through personal contact with his men keeps the trains rolling and the rails smooth.

Although we chat easily with various McCloud employes, we find that the greatest source of local history is pioneer McCloud railroader and No. 1 Conductor, Charlie Haines.

Charlie is a genial sort with an appreciation of a good story and his years on the McCloud have given him plenty of material. But, his greatest interest, outside of the railroad, perhaps, is a little dog called Speck. Speck is a smart little fox terrier and (I hope she is still alive) certainly worth a few lines here. In fact if Mark Twain had been writing this it's almost certain he would have called the piece: "Charlie Haines and The Swearing Dog of McCloud."

Yes, Charlie's dog actually swears. Unbelievable as it may sound this curious fact is demonstrated when her master uses an oath to express his opinion. When this occurs, and it does frequently on a railroad, the little dog immediately joins in with a series of sharp, rapid barks that must indeed be profane in dog language. Throughout any other type of English, no matter how heated, she remains absolutely quiet. Recalling a few words of our own we found that it worked equally well with anyone who might care to match profanity with this raildog.

Speck has other and more commendable talents which come to light when Charlie takes her car checking. Since this has become a matter of nightly recreation for the little terrier she knows the route by heart and if Charlie should miss a car or fail to take the right route Speck promptly informs him by means of a series of sharp barks which may or may not be obscene. And so to any collector of raildog stories, I submit, Speck, the swearing dog of McCloud.

The history of the McCloud River Railroad is to a great extent the history of the lumbering activity in the region because the two industries grew up together. In fact when the railroad first started back in 1897 it was merely another logging road. In those days the mill was located farther west at Upton. Eventually as the logging operations advanced the lumberjacks found themselves well on the eastern side of Mount Shasta. Since Upton was left behind and the greatest activity, by far, lay ahead it was decided to move the entire outfit, mill and all, east of Shasta. This was the beginning of the town of McCloud.

The entire output of the new mill at McCloud was shipped out by rail to Upton and what was once the site of the big mill was now merely the transfer point where the loads were turned over to the Southern Pacific. In 1906, when the lumber railroad built into Sisson (now known as Mount Shasta City), that point was made the junction point and little Upton faded off the map completely.

More rail construction was begun in 1907 when the rails moved into the forest east of McCloud. A steady stream of logs now rolled into town on this new line and after a brief lay-over departed on west bound trains as finished lumber. 1907 was also the year the little backwoods railroad began to really grow up, for this was the year the first oil-burning locomotive appeared on the McCloud and almost at once woodburners were a thing of the past. It was also in 1907 that the road became a common carrier and assumed its place as the McCloud River Railroad Company.

The Pacific Gas and Electric Company came to notice

the McCloud River Railroad in 1922 and it was called upon to play an important part in the construction of the Pit #1 and Pit #3 power houses as well as the Pit #4 dam and diversion tunnels. During this activity all of the material and machinery was carried over the rails of the McCloud River Railroad.

From a point on the McCloud's main line known as Bartle, the railroad built a 5.3 mile spur and from the end of this spur the P. G. & E. built a private railroad to the power sites. Formally called the Mt. Shasta Corporation Construction Railroad in the power company's records it is still remembered locally as the Pit River Railroad. The line ran through the Cayton Valley and up the river to the Pit No. 1 power house site. Later a branch was extended ten miles more to Pit No. 3 and later still further to Pit No. 4. Although long since abandoned, the rotting ties can still be seen from U. S. Highway 299.

Additional railroad construction came in 1931 when the Great Northern connected with the Western Pacific up in the McCloud country. At this time an extension was put through which allowed the McCloud River Railroad to connect with these two railroads. Upon completion of this connecting link a huge celebration was held—complete with special trains to "end o' track," which in this case was the junction with the Great Northern. Here a committee of dignitaries commemorated the Great Northern's long heralded entry into California. But that accomplishment of high finance and engineering didn't impress the local delegates nearly as much as the fact that the McCloud River Railroad had connected with *both* of the larger roads. This now gave the McCloud railroad interchange with three major lines, the Southern Pacific at Mt. Shasta, at the western end of the line, and the Great Northern and Western Pacific at its eastern end. Truly something for a short line to celebrate. (Actual interchange is made with the Great Northern at Lookout. The Western Pacific takes over from the Big "G" at Bieber, 11 miles south of Lookout.)

But even as this is being written an even larger celebration is being planned on the McCloud River Railroad. This time the occasion will be the completion of a 32 mile, million and a half dollar extension into Burney, Shasta County.

The new Burney extension leaves the McCloud River Railroad at Bear Flat, a junction point on the main line, between Pondosa and Bartle. For ten miles, between Bear Flat and Ditch Creek, the new line uses a rebuilt logging spur acquired from the McCloud Lumber Company. At Ditch Creek 22 miles of brand new railroad actually begins, using in some places the old P. G. & E. "Pit River Railroad" roadbed.

Grading began in the spring of 1954 and rail laying was under way by August. Later that month track reached the Cayton Valley and before the first of November revenue freight was originating from this point.

Not far beyond Cayton Valley the railroad crosses Lake Britton on a seven-span deck girder bridge. Although the early winter snows halted the graders on the opposite bank, the steel work on the bridge itself continued throughout the winter. Early in December tragedy touched the Lake Britton job. The main span had just been placed in position when suddenly without warning it plunged into the icy water of the lake, carrying a workman to his death.

The $300,000 steel bridge was finally completed without further incident and the track work was resumed at the first sign of spring.

Directly responsible for the new railroad is the fact that the McCloud Lumber Company recently purchased a tract in the Burney Basin containing one-and-a-half-billion board feet of timber. This stand, acquired from the Fruit Growers' Supply Company, is expected to last for 20 to 25 years. In addi-

Winter 1953, McCloud River Railroad.

Wood burner No. 9 running light on the McCloud about 1910.

Photo courtesy Randolph Brandt

No. 8 brings in a train of logs.

Photo courtesy Randolph Brandt

Early steam tractor used in the McCloud area.

"Log jammer" loading railroad cars.

tion there is a total of five to six billion board feet available in the area that will eventually be logged; so it is reasonable to expect to see the McCloud River Railroad hauling logs to McCloud for the next 50 years anyway. With this amount of tonnage, along with the output of the mills in the Burney area, it is little wonder that the front office experts fully expect the construction costs of the new road to be repaid within thirty years out of revenue originating in the Burney area.

As you can see the Burney extension is by no means a temporary piece of track designed to exploit the area and be written off. Actually the roadbed is solidly constructed with creosoted ties and good 85 and 90 pound relay rail from the Fruit Growers' Supply Company Camp Harvey logging road and the Santa Fe. Ballast is the familiar crushed red lava used by the McCloud River Railroad and other railroads in the Mount Shasta area.

From Burney a five or six mile spur will serve the Scott Lumber Company's mill. The Scott people are old customers of the McCloud River Railroad, having several logging spurs connecting elsewhere with the McCloud River Railroad.

The new Burney line was officially opened on July 3, 1955 with appropriate golden spike ceremonies at Burney. The first train ever to visit Burney brought many people interested in seeing this event. Visitors came from Seattle, Portland, Los Angeles and San Diego and a dozen other places. Railfans, officials, newspaper men and photographers were all there. A special train ran from the Bay Area to Burney with several hundred passengers all eager to witness the completion of the first major railroad extension to be built in Northern California by private capital in the past 25 years.

At the present time passengers are carried by company operated buses and LCL freight, mail and express are hauled by company trucks, but there was a time when the railroad was the only dependable method of entering this wild country. Passenger traffic was then a regular and an important part of the McCloud schedule, but there's no need to go into the old story of automobiles and better roads at this time. Suffice it to say that during the period of transition the rails became more accustomed to the rattle of the freight car than the muffled click of the passenger coach. Occasionally a special train with William Randolph Hearst and a party of celebrities would come in on the McCloud River Railroad bound for the Hearst Estate at Wyntoon.

Perhaps the last bid for passenger revenue came in 1930 when, following the example of other railroads throughout the country, the Southern Pacific and the McCloud River Railroad organized a ski trip into the Shasta snow fields. The skiers arrived at Mount Shasta City aboard the S.P. alright, but the good people of that town met the special and offered to personally show their guests around in automobiles. It must have been a great blow for the McCloud's management when their ski special left Mount Shasta City with only two passengers aboard. One of these was a railroad man deadheading back to McCloud and the other we'll wager was a railfan. Ever since that fateful day the McCloud River Railroad has devoted its rails to FREIGHT SERVICE ONLY.

But as a freight line it's not doing half bad and boasts a rather impressive roster of rolling stock . . . and with 14 locomotives (8 steam, 6 Diesel), 305 company owned cars and 98 miles of track things can get pretty busy. As a concrete example of how busy things can get here are the ton-miles figures for five years:

> 1950—20,690,000
> 1951—23,154,000
> 1952—14,524,000
> 1953—17,853,000
> 1954—22,864,000.

These figures are, of course, without the Burney extension which should add additional tonnage in the years to come.

The esprit de corps is high among the McCloud employes and their sense of pride is admirable. Stories of smash-ups and derailments are hard to find because the railroaders seem to feel that the publishing of such a yarn would be bad publicity for the line and perhaps reflect upon their integrity as railroad men. Even pictures of old equipment were reluctantly loaned because it was feared that people would receive the impression that the railroad was still operating antiquated equipment.

There was one mishap, however, they are still talking about on the McCloud—that's the big snow of 1937-38. You can still hear stories of that eventful winter told in various versions from the president's office down to the pits in the roundhouse, but regardless of where you hear it you will gather that it was quite a blow. Former President P. N. Meyers was superintendent then and he and Charlie Haines were out on the line in the thick of it; so this is their version:

If you wish to consult the weather bureau records for the winter of 1937-38 you'll find that it was an extra tough one all over California. It rained for weeks with hardly a let-up. Creeks and rivers that for years had carried little more than a trickle suddenly became raging torrents. Floods were frequent in the low lands, but up in the mountains this cycle of bad weather brought snow, snow and more snow! The McCloud River trains tried valiantly to keep the line open, but it seemed as fast as the snow plows could clear the track old man winter was right behind to cover them up again.

The railroad didn't own a rotary plow as all previous snows had been managed with their Russell plows. (The Russell plow is perhaps the best known of all push plows. It was first used on the Intercolonial Railway of Canada in

1885. The plow itself resembles the bow of a ship and, as the name implies, the operation consists mainly of PUSH. Bucking snow with these plows is no job for a cautious person. Since brute force, in the form of two, four or even more locomotives is the driving power behind a push plow, it requires a great deal of experience and no little daring to hit a bank of snow at just the right speed.) Plowing snow with any type of plow is dangerous business at best, however the road had to be kept open or McCloud would be completely snowed in from all sides.

It was under these conditions that the regular east bound train left McCloud. "East bound freight cleared McCloud yards" was the message that went out on the wires and the dispatcher sat back to wait. North McCloud, Ash Creek Junction and Esperanza were passed without incident. So far so good. But then came delay. At first the dispatcher wrote "late" after the train number, but then as time wore on "late" became "unreported'. Frantically he called every little way station and section house that had a wire, but the train could not be located. Somewhere out in that vast wilderness of white an entire train and its crew were hopelessly stranded.

Aboard the lost train the situation was getting desperate. Their only chance to reach civilization was to keep going the way their snow plow pointed . . . straight ahead! The two locomotives would repeatedly run at the blockade of snow that lay between them and safety and each time the blow sent a crashing shiver through the entire train as the 13 foot plow futilely tried to batter the 18 foot snowfall. To make matters worse the oil and water were getting low in the engines. In a last desperate attempt to keep up a fire wood was cut from the trees sticking up through the snow and the oilburners tried their best to operate on the wet wood. For water snow was shoveled into the tanks to be melted by live steam. It was a losing battle. The steam pressure was going down and the danger of freezing to death now seemed unbelievably close.

In the meantime Superintendent Meyers, a doctor and a party of men were battling the storm with three locomotives and another Russell plow. Time after time the three engines would rush headlong into that wall of snow only to make a minor indentation, then reverse, back up and repeat the process. Their goal was measured in miles, but their progress could be measured only in feet. It was during this necessarily rough handling of equipment that one of their number lost his life when he was thrown under the grinding wheels of the train.

Finally they reached the stricken train, but they were hardly in a position to act as a rescue party. The snow had piled up behind them and return was impossible. The rescued and the rescuers now found themselves in exactly the same predicament. Together they made their way to a section house where a track worker and his family stayed, and here, under 18 feet of snow, fifty stranded railroad men and a Mexican family lived on tortillas and what little else they could scrape up to keep alive.

It was five days later when another snow plow, with every remaining locomotive the road owned behind it, came through the snow and brought the snowbound crews back to McCloud.

No, it'll be some time before the boys on the McCloud River Railroad forget the big snow of 1937-38, the winter that tied the road up so completely that every locomotive on the line and every available man was drafted into a gigantic battle with the elements.

Winter comes to the McCloud River Railroad.

On September 15, 1941, the McCloud River Railroad celebrated its connection with the Great Northern and the Great Northern goat helped No. 19 get a train load of forest products started on its way to market.

When the McCloud River Railroad officially joined the Great Northern on September 15, 1931, 57 loads of lumber were sent out via the Big "G". On November 10, 1931, 76 loads were sent out via the Western Pacific. (No. 19, shown at the head end) was nicknamed "Pedro" because of previous service in Mexico where she picked up bullet marks during a revolution.

Photo courtesy McCloud Lumber Co.

A typical McCloud River Railroad train. Photo taken 1946 on the flat lands east of McCloud.

Photo by Curtis Ingram

Round house at McCloud 1946.

Photo by Curtis Ingrum

Some McCloud railroaders. Left to right: K. C. Smith, S. J. Schuyler, Frank Facchin, L. C. Miller, M. E. Delgado, Vince Huckabay and A. N. Carter.

No. 27 gets a general overhaul in the back shop at McCloud.

Mt. Shasta from McCloud, California.

Log pond and mill of the McCloud Lumber Company.

An old photo of No. 8 and a logging train. Curved trestle has since become a fill.

Photo courtesy C. M. Haines

The McCloud River Railroad still operates one of the few remaining switchbacks. This photo taken at the switchback shows turntable built on stilts used to turn snow plows.

Photo by Jack R. Wagner

TECRASILK PHOTO

McCloud River Railroad cabooses.

Photo by Jack R. Wagner

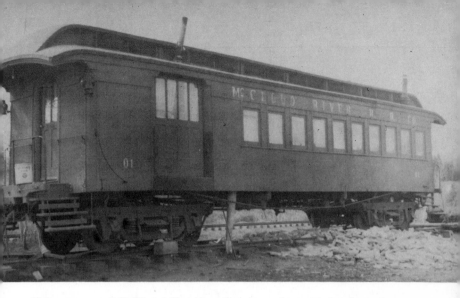

This veteran of McCloud River passenger service ends its days as a section car.

TECRASILK PHOTO

The first No. 17 was a Shay built by Lima in 1911.

From an old post card

This "Siamese Twin" arrangement was designed for the steep grade between Upton and McCloud. It was a Vauclain (cross) compound built by Baldwin in 1900. Later, the double-ender was separated to make two locomotives, the No. 5 and 6. No. 6 was purchased by the Atkinson Construction Company and was stored by them at San Leandro for years. The lower photo was taken while the engine was engaged in construction work at Treasure Island, San Francisco Bay in 1937.

TECRASILK PHOTO

No. 16, a McCloud "Mike" stops for a drink of water.

April, 1940.

TECRASILK PHOTO

No. 18 was for a long time the "show" engine of the road. During the Panama-Pacific International Exposition in San Francisco in 1915, it was placed on display.

On the turntable at McCloud.

Built in 1915, this 2-8-0 came to the McCloud River Railroad from the Copper River & Northwestern Railroad of Alaska.

McCloud River No. 27 just after it had been recieved from the Copper River & Northwestern in November, 1938. It was the No. 73 of the Alaska road.

TECRASILK PHOTO

Laying steel on the 32 mile, million and a half dollar extension into Burney, Shasta County, California. This branch was completed in July, 1955.

Photo courtesy Flake Willis

Part of the Burney extension, the 500 foot Lake Britton Bridge cost $300,000 and the life of one man.

Rails into Burney. The first major railroad extension to be built in Northern California by private capital in the past 25 years.

The big snow of 1937-38, the winter that tied the road up so completely that every locomotive on the line and every available man was drafted into a gigantic battle with the elements.

Photo courtesy C. M. Haines

CHAPTER IV

ALL'S QUIET ON THE QUINCY

MANY DRAMATIC STORIES have been told of railroading and railroad construction, tales of blood spilled along the right-of-way with every mile post a monument to violent death; tales of huge fortunes dwindled by unforeseen difficulties and battles with the elements; stories of racing locomotives and blazing bridges; of heroes and villains; presidents and hobos. Yes, numerous legends and ballads have come to us as gems of Americana from the main line, but if that's the type of action you require then you'll be disappointed in this chapter. However, if you can slow down and come in off the "high iron," forget the whistle that wails in the night and the thunder of the huge road engine then this is written for you.

Picture, if you can, a sleepy little mountain town with wooded hills rising from each end of its main street. Not far from town is a green carpeted valley where livestock wanders leisurely about and an occasional deer or even a bear can be seen hurrying across the clearing to the protection of the woods on the other side. In the center of this bucolic scene, and the only sign of civilization, is a freight train of about

six or seven assorted cars being pulled by a diminutive locomotive. The cars rock independently from side to side giving
the little train a somewhat uneven appearance. Presently the
consist approaches a trestle, and while its progress seemed
slow before, we notice the locomotive easing out onto the
structure at little more than a snail's pace. All hands are now
leaning from the cab, looking down into the stream and
pointing at what seems to be the very underpinning of the
bridge. Conversation is excited and the air seems tense. But
don't worry, the bridge isn't about to collapse and even if it
were no one would give it a thought as all attention is now
turned to the speckled beauties swimming in Greenhorn
Creek. This is life on the Quincy, the line that has my vote
as the friendliest and most informal railroad in the country.

Some time ago, in an article I wrote for "Railroad Magazine," I attempted to explain how mail intended for the Chicago, Burlington & Quincy Railroad, but addressed simply to:
"The Quincy" (as some eastern railroaders persist in calling the
C. B. & Q.), ends up in Quincy, California. Looking for a
different way to open the article, I wrote it as an "open letter" to Mr. Ralph Budd, president of the C. B. & Q. The
general wording was to the effect that if Mr. Budd ever won-
dered why mail sometimes comes to his office in the Burlington Building marked "sent to Quincy, Calif. by mistake" my
article should help to clear things up. I explained that Quincy
was a small town in the Feather River section of California
and Mr. Budd and his 9,000 mile C. B. & Q. would never
have been put to this inconvenience if there didn't happen
to be a six mile short line out here called the Quincy Railroad. I even ventured to say that Mr. Budd had probably
never heard of it or the town of Quincy for that matter.

Needless to say I was quite pleased when my "open
letter" was answered by a very friendly, personal letter from
Ralph Budd in which he informed me that he had indeed

heard of Quincy, having spent some time in this part of the country while working on reconnaissance for the "Inside Gateway" which the Great Northern and Western Pacific finally built from Klamath Falls to Keddie in 1931. Mr. Budd's recollections were very interesting and indicated that he, also, was much impressed with the wild beauty of this area.

The "boys" who operate the "little Quincy" are just about the greatest bunch of railroaders you've ever seen. Nearly all of them have held good jobs on larger railroads, but like a big time newspaper man turned country editor, they have preferred to live in the quiet and contentment of a small town.

Take L. H. Thayer, for instance, who until his retirement on December 31, 1954, was superintendent, assistant treasurer and director of the Quincy Railroad Company. Thayer is a veteran of 50 years of railroad service with the last 31 spent with the Quincy. He started out with the old Colorado Midland, which went out of business shortly after the close of World War I and is still remembered as the world's most extensive railroad abandonment. After that Thayer joined the Denver & Rio Grande and later the Western Pacific. Joining the Quincy Railroad in 1923 he soon found that the little road offered plenty of interest and was good for the sense of humor as well. As a result Thayer could take or make a joke about the little railroad with equal felicity, but through it all it was plain to see that he never once lost his fondness and respect for the short line.

Upon Thayer's retirement Orville A. Meyers, for 13 years station agent on the Quincy, was given the well deserved promotion to superintendent and the road continues to be managed by careful and experienced hands. Meyers' devotion to the railroad was apparent when he was agent and it's safe to say that no better superintendent could have been found anywhere. But Meyers' knows the price he paid for his promotion every time the town fire alarm sounds. He used to be a member of the local hose company and responded to all calls. Now, with the added responsibilities, it is no longer possible to be so readily available.

The new agent is E. M. Thompson, a resident of Quincy for most of his life and was formerly employed by the Quincy Railroad as agent from 1934 to 1937.

I remember J. F. Moody very well because at the age of 74, when I first met him in 1946, he was the railroad's only conductor and the town's only undertaker. He also held the position of coroner until that job was consolidated with the Plumas County Sheriff's Office. Moody's railroad career (prior to 1916) included the Southern Pacific, the Carson & Colorado (the narrow gauge offspring of the Virginia & Truckee) and the Oregon Short Line, which later became the Union Pacific's Portland route, but his last thirty working years he devoted to conducting funerals and trains in and around Quincy. Moody retired in July 1947 and died in 1954 at the age of 82.

Ed Lonkey was another well known Quincy character. Ed was born in 1877 in Virginia City and could tell many wild tales of the old days in that roaring mining town. Although he didn't work for the historic Virginia & Truckee, Ed could well remember when that railroad ran 50 scheduled trains a day! Ed was a good engineer in his day and pulled throttle on the Verdi Lumber Railroad and the famous Tonopah & Goldfield Railroad. He was also an engineer on the Quincy Railroad up to the time they retired the faithful old steam locomotive and bought a Diesel. Ed then announced that he would never touch the critter and promptly became a brakeman. Ed's religious vow never to so much as touch the throttle added fuel, even in Quincy, to the argument of Diesel versus steam. Ed's other chief characteristic was his steadfast refusal to be photographed. The only known picture of Ed Lonkey shows nothing but a streak as he quickly turned his caboose end toward the camera. Ed Lonkey retired in November 1948 and died in February 1955. He was 77.

If you ever get up in that part of the country, be sure you talk to Solon F. Luzzader. He's the engineer on the Quincy Railroad and is as fine a fellow as you'd want to know. He learned all about the insides of locomotives at the Southern Pacific shops in Oakland and later he was an engineer on the defunct Indian Valley Line that ran to Englemine in Plumas County, California. In fact he brought the last train out of Engelmine in 1938 and when he pulled off his gloves both he and the railroad were through. The road went to the junk man and Solon went to the Quincy where you'll find him now. Although still a little partial to steam himself, Solon makes efficient use of the Quincy's Diesel locomotive . . . even to the point of keeping warm a can of salted peanuts which he freely extends as his contribution to the railroad's hospitality.

Perhaps you are wondering just what a railroad only six miles long does for a living and how it happened to get there in the first place. Well, there is a story behind the Quincy Railroad. Maybe it's not the kind you expect, but there's a story nevertheless.

The need for a railroad at Quincy dates back to the announcement made by Chief Engineer Bogue of the Western Pacific when he stated emphatically that the newest of the transcontinental routes would adhere to a 1% maximum grade. This meant that when the line was built up through the Feather River Canyon it would be necessary to by-pass the town of Quincy by some six miles and at a higher level!

Quincy, the county seat of Plumas County, was situated in one of the most isolated sections of the state, without even a good wagon road. Then suddenly it blossomed with activity as the railroad surveyors arrived, followed in time by the graders and the rail gangs. Quincy began to take on the appearances of a boom town as strangers in the form of dark, foreign looking laborers, burly tunnel drivers and khaki clad engineers flocked into town. Livestock and mules slushed through the muddy streets on their way to end o' track. By now the work trains were within whistling distance. And so it was that in the local barber shops, saloons and general stores the main topic of conversation was the coming of the railroad.

No one seems to have questioned the engineering standards of the Western Pacific, which were responsible for keeping that railroad from entering Quincy, but it was becoming increasingly evident that if the community was to be benefitted at all by the new railroad there would have to be some way to coax business in from the main line. The townspeople now began to talk of a short line, a railroad of their own, that would connect them with the Western Pacific.

It was in 1908 that one J. J. Rutledge floated into town. He was a suave, businesslike man who soon got himself introduced to the local citizenry and immediately became the leader of the local railway bosters. Mr. Rutledge, who every now and then dropped a hint that he had influential friends in San Francisco and Oakland, suggested that the local people show their enthusiasm and support the proposed short line by raising some of the money among themselves with the understanding that he would secure the balance. His suggestion was acted upon and subscriptions in the form of notes were taken with the stipulation that when Mr. Rutledge secured the investment of sufficient outside capital these notes would be turned over to the corporation to be formed.

As a safety precaution a local committee headed by H. C. Flourney was appointed to see that the interests of the people were protected.

American Locomotive Works Photo

Locomotive No. 1 of the Quincy (Western) Railroad. Built in 1910 by the American Locomotive Works she was sold in July 1947 to become a stationary boiler at a cedar mill near Quincy.

No. 2 was purchased new in 1924 and is still used as a standby. This combination coach, purchased second hand from the S. P. for use on the Quincy, was finally retired to become a section shed.

Photos courtesy Leonard Thayer

The town of Quincy, California, and the American Valley. Western
Pacific main line can be seen at the top of photo.

Quincy in winter.

J. H. Eastman photos

BOTH ENDS OF THE LINE

Quincy station and General Office.

Quincy Junction may be just a mile post to the Western Pacific, but it's the eastern terminus of the Quincy Railroad.

Photos by Jack R. Wagner

QUINCY JUNCTION

In due time Mr. Rutledge organized what was called the Quincy & Eastern Railway Company and promptly elected himself and two of his big city friends as three of the five directors. After this was neatly done he next made a demand upon Mr. Flourney for the surrender of the notes. This request was refused by Mr. Flourney and his committe until a guarantee was given that funds enough to complete the railroad had been placed on deposit. Mr. Rutledge, it seems, didn't have such funds. The locals, who proved to be more than a match for the promoter, immediately took steps to oust the three out of town directors and to recover the books and other properties.

Apparently pressure was applied in the right places because a small newspaper item printed in April 1909 reports simply that the board of directors of the Quincy & Eastern Railroad met and accepted the "resignation" of Mr. J. J. Rutledge and his associates. The vacancies were promptly filled with local men. One of the new directors was Mr. A. W. Keddie, a man who first came into prominence when he agitated for wagon roads into Plumas County and later "sold" the Western Pacific on the present Feather River Route. Mr. Keddie, needless to say, was somewhat of a local hero and his addition to the directorate brought considerable prestige to the corporation.

There also joined the group at this time, another railroad promoter by the name of John Sexton. (After four years with the Quincy Railroad Mr. Sexton went to Nevada where he succeeded in putting the Eureka Nevada on a paying basis and gained considerable renown when he gained the upper hand in a crossing dispute with the Central Pacific. His strategy consisted of simply building a red picket fence across the C. P. right of way and demanding that the big road unlock and lock the gate for every train. They soon grew tired of this and came to terms.) Mr. Sexton was a huge, two fisted man who had a way of getting things done. He quickly estimated that it would require $30,000 to build and equip the railroad.

In April of 1909 there were 25 stockholders and by June of that same year the number had grown to 65 with some $54,000 pledged. On Thursday evening July 8, at a stockholder's meeting at the Odd Fellows Hall, it was found that the response had been more than adequate and the following resolution was passed:

> RESOLVED: that the directors of the Quincy & Eastern Railway Company are hereby advised and directed to begin at the earliest date practicable the construction and equipment of a broad gauge steam railroad from a connection with the Western Pacific at Hartwell Station (now known as Quincy Junction) into the town of Quincy, to the end that said broad gauge railroad shall be completed and equipped for operation on or before January 1, 1910."

An investigation of the labor market at the time showed that foreign labor (Greek) could be had for $1.80 a day without board while American home laborers worked for $2.50 a day, also without meals. It was decided to use American labor throughout. And so the contracts were placed and construction begun.

It wasn't a difficult piece of building, being all level with the exception of the "last mile" which rises out of the American Valley and ascends to the Western Pacific main line via a 4% grade. But even that was a straightforward job of grading with an occasional cut through easily moved earth.

Soon the equipment began to arrive. First the rail, followed in short order by the rolling stock. (Newspaper accounts at the time stated that the rail was 50 pound relay purchased from the S. P. for $32 a ton delivered to Marysville from the Woodland-Red Bluff section which was then going to 70 pound rail. The Quincy Railroad records, however, maintain that at least a part of the rail used was 52 pound from the old Boca & Loyalton RR.)

The rolling stock consisted of a flat car and a combination baggage car and passenger coach purchased from the Southern Pacific. Finally there came from the American Locomotive Company the little Quincy No. 1, a 37 ton steam locomotive with a small tender built on the engine frame and supported by a four wheel truck. This arrangement gave the little engine the wheel classification of O-4-4T.

It was about 11:30 on the morning of that big day late in 1909 when Superintendent Sexton had his workers lay the last rail in place. Local Attorney L. N. Peter, who also held the position of vice-president of the road, drove the last spike to the accompaniment of the Court House and Hose Company bells and the Quincy Brass Band.

When things had quieted down a little, A. W. Keddie, who by this time was called the "father of the Western Pacific route through Plumas County," was called upon for a few remarks. Afterward the good ladies of Quincy rushed forward with a free lunch for the railroad laborers who had so bravely laid rail through the pastures and meadows of the American Valley. The rest of the day was occupied by free rides on the newly completed railroad.

The official name of the line had been changed from the Quincy & Eastern of Mr. Rutledge's day to the Quincy Western, a title that was soon to be corrupted as the "Quick & Windy."

By the summer of 1910 the outside world seems to have heard of the Quincy Western and numerous excursions arrived and left via the local railroad, but unfortunately for the public spirited organizers and investors the line wasn't much of a financial success. In October 1910, when the railroad was hardly a year old, the revenue amounted to only $35 a day, but the management continued to hold out until 1917. At this time the end of their financial rope was reached and the Quincy Western went into receivership. Although the original stock was worthless, the railroad was saved from the junk man by the F. S. Murphy Lumber Company, which acquired the property as a necessary accessory to their lumber mill. A complete reorganization took place and the Quincy again had its name changed. This time it became merely The Quincy Railroad Company. Some stock was sold in the town of Quincy as a jesture, but most of the shares remained in the hands of the lumber company.

In 1926 the Murphy Company sold the mill in a transaction that also included the former company's interest in the railroad. And so the situation remains today, with the mill, now known as the Quincy Lumber Company, owning about 90% and the remaining 10% held by the townspeople. Regardless of the lumber company's "lion's share" the little railroad is operated separate and apart and to all intents and purpose the mill is regarded as just a good customer.

The heaviest single hauling job handled by the Quincy was during the construction of the Bucks Ranch Dam (1925-1927). At that time most of the materials and equipment arrived via the Quincy Railroad. Contractors' equipment such as a locomotive and a string of dump cars as well as power shovels of all kinds made their way over the light rail of the Quincy Railroad. Largest of all the shovels was a huge Marion railway shovel weighing 221,000 pounds. During the project some twenty-five steam and gasoline operated shovels rolled safely over the Quincy Railroad.

Passenger service was first maintained with the already mentioned combination car which was merely coupled to the regular freight train. After a while, however, this creeking but picturesque car was retired from road service to spend the rest of its life as a section shed.

This being the motor age there then appeared on the Quincy a strange contraption. It was a gasoline motor car that pulled a 20-passenger coach. This conveyance soon earned for itself the name "galloping goose."

The new addition made the passenger and express department operate separately and independent of the freight train—a fact that had its disadvantages as well as its advantages. The Quincy now became a two train railroad! This, of course, put an added burden on the dispatching system, but this was handled quite well over the private telephone line to the junction. That is, things worked well until one day the engineer of the outgoing freight decided that he could make the run to the junction before the "galloping goose" even got started. This error of judgment resulted in the little railroad's first and only cornfield meet, an event that involved the only two trains on the road.

The motor car was patched up and ran for a time even after Superintendent Thayer took over; but eventually it was abandoned to become a hamburger joint in Quincy, a purpose it served until it was destroyed by fire to no one's great sorrow.

At the present time passengers are met at Quincy Junction by a sedan although there is an application before the Public Utilities Commission for permission to discontinue all passenger service. It is expected that the railroad will soon operate for "freight service only" and with only one train on the rails the possibility of headon collisions is considered remote indeed.

Some of the older movie fans might be interested to know that when Jack Pickford was making his silent masterpiece, "Valley of the Wolf" in the Feather River country,

Quincy was his headquarters and cars and equipment traveled over the Quincy Railroad.

Former Superintendent Thayer recalls that the movie company had a Western Pacific engine and crew at their disposal to take over the company's cars at the junction and pull them up the canyon to location. One cloudy day Pickford dismissed the W. P. crew and his actors and technicians returned to Quincy. That afternoon the sun peeked out from behind the clouds and, anxious to get in a few more hours of shooting, the director tried in vain to get in touch with the Western Pacific engine crew. Finally he asked Thayer if a Quincy locomotive could take them all the way up to location, which would mean going out on the W. P. main line. The superintendent, with typical Quincy accommodation, replied, "Sure, it's all right with me, but I doubt if the Western Pacific would like it."

As for present revenue the Quincy supplies the State Division of Highways, the local oil companies, the Forestry Service and brings in such LCL freight that comes by rail to local business houses. The large shippers are, of course, the lumber mills and direct spur connection is made to the five major producers. (The Quincy Lumber Co., Meadow Valley Lumber Co., The Essex Lumber Co., The Calvada Lumber Co., and the Mason & Hager Lumber Co.).

Twice a day switching service and two connections with the Western Pacific gives the mills better service than they would get if they were on the main line, a fact that keeps the Quincy Railroad in good standing with the customers.

As for the future of the road, it pretty much depends on the fate of the car load shippers. Fortunately some of the mills are on a sustained yield basis, which means that they have enough forest land available and are cutting on a scientific plan that will make their operation last indefinitely.

However, some of the smaller mills cannot do this and when their timber allocation is used up they're through.

Then there's that ever present mountain hazard—forest fire! Recently one single fire reduced the life of one mill by five years when it destroyed over 50,000,000 feet of timber. Even now the fate of the Quincy Railroad, as well as the matchless beauty of the country around it, may be in the hands of some careless camper or hunter.

And there's the story of the Quincy Railroad Company. As you have seen it's not a very large company and they don't make a lot of money, but as a tributary that flows into the main stream it is certainly deserving of its place on the roster of American Railroads.

Burlington Lines

Chicago, Burlington & Quincy Railroad Company
The Colorado and Southern Railway Company
Fort Worth and Denver City Railway Company
The Wichita Valley Railway Company

Burlington Route

547 West Jackson Boulevard
Chicago, Illinois   6

Ralph Budd
President

June 5, 1947

Mr. Jack R. Wagner,
Care Railroad Magazine,
205 East 42nd Street,
New York, 17, New York.

Dear Mr. Wagner:

Your Open Letter to me published in the Railroad
Magazine for July 1947 is amusing and informative, it recalls
very vividly some of my early experiences.

My first visit to Quincy, California, was in the
fall of 1909, about the time the Western Pacific track was
being completed through the Feather River Canyon.   I went
by stage from Oroville, and was around that country for
some little time working on the reconnaissance for the
railroad which the Great Northern and Western Pacific
finally built from Klamath Falls to Keddie in 1931.   We
had several different routes by which the Western Pacific
could be reached from the north, all very rugged approaching
the connection in Feather River Canyon.

I am glad to have this up to date report on the
little "Q" of California.

Yours sincerely,

Ralph Budd

Former engineer J. C. Laughlin.

Railroad conductor and town undertaker, the late J. F. Moody.

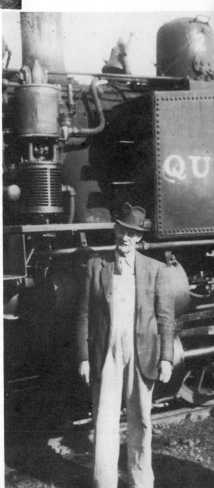

General Office staff in 1941. Left to right: Bernice Wright, secretary; L. H. Thayer, superintendent; Orville A Myers, agent; John Doane, former agent. When Mr. Thayer retired Orville Myers became superintendent of the Quincy Railroad.

Operating personnel circa 1941: J. C. Laughlin, engineer; Lloyd Stevenson, brakeman; J. H. Moody, conductor, and M. E. Kelsey, fireman.

Photo courtesy L. H. Thayer

No. 1 as she appeared after 37 years of service. Shortly after this photo was taken she was retired.

The No. 2 was the "work horse" of the Quincy until the road acquired the Diesel-electric (No. 3) in 1945.

TECRASILK PHOTOS

Photos by Jack R. Wagner

No. 3 at work and ''at home''.

Engineer Solon Luzzader formerly pulled throttle on the defunct Indian Valley line. In fact he brought the last train out of Englemine in 1938. When he pulled off his gloves both he and the railroad were through.

Although still a little partial to steam, Solon makes efficient use of the Quincy Diesel.

Photos by Jack R. Wagner

Former Superintnedent L. H. Thayer. (Sept. 1946)

Below: Yards and shops at Quincy.

Photos by Jack R. Wagner

Photos courtesy L. H. Thayer

Quincy RR section foreman taking his noon nap
No. 2 and train crossing the American Valley.

The Quincy RR No. 3 is
a 380 h.p. Diesei-electric
built by American.

Livestock on the li

Quincy Railroad Company

Time Table No. 35

(Cancels Time Table No. 34)

EFFECTIVE 12:01 A.M. JUNE 2nd, 1946.

READ DOWN					READ UP	
1	3		TRAIN NOS.		2	4
6:30 A.M.	7:45 P.M.	Lv	Quincy	Ar	7:30 A.M.	8:45 P.M.
7:00 A.M.	8:05 P.M.	Ar	Quincy Junction	Lv	7:10 A.M.	8:20 P.M.

Train No. 1 meets Western Pacific Train No. 1, due at Quincy Junction 7:07 A.M.

Train No. 3 meets Western Pacific Train No. 2, due at Quincy Junction 8:15 P. M.

Western Pacific Passenger Trains Nos. 1 & 2 make regular stop at Quincy Junction.

The Company reserves the right to vary from the above time as circumstances may require.

Quincy, California

Issued by: L. H. Thayer, Supt.

Quincy Railroad Company

Motor Coach Time Table No. 20

(Cancels Time Schedule No. 19)

Superseded

Issued May 10, 1946.
Effective June 2nd, 1946.

Service rendered is operated in lieu of rail service, if and when, rail service is not performed.

READ DOWN						READ UP	
3	1			Schedule Nos.		2	4
P.M.	A.M.	Miles		Stations		A.M.	P.M.
7:45	6:30	0	Lv	Quincy	Ar	7:30	8:45
8:05	7:00	5	Ar	Quincy Junction	Lv	7:10	8:20

TERMINALS

QUINCY JUNCTION: — W. P. R. R. CO. DEPOT
QUINCY: — QUINCY R. R. CO. DEPOT

Quincy, California

Issued by: L. H. Thayer, Supt.

CHAPTER V

THE STEEL TRAIL TO THE MOTHER LODE

IF YOU HAVE EVER TOURED the picturesque towns and land-marks of California's Mother Lode or if you have read any of Bret Harte's famous stories of the mining towns and are familiar with the western adventures of Mark Twain you'll have a good understanding and insight into the country we are about to visit. But, if you haven't, then a line drawn on your map due east of San Francisco will take you into the western foothills of the Sierra Nevada Mountains and Tuolumne County .

For the greater part the surface of this area is that of rolling foothills broken occasionally by volcanic formations. As progress is made eastward the mountains become higher and the valleys smaller until the snowy heights of the high Sierra are reached. Through this country runs the "Mother Lode," that famous quartz formation that has been the source of vast fortunes and for a time was the principal lure of the west. It is in this historic section of granite boulders, red dirt and pine trees that we find the Sierra Railroad.

It was by a curious and roundabout way that the people of Tuolumne County first learned of the proposed railroad.

A piece of news had been turned up by the investigation of the suicide of one Albert L. Stetson, as reported in the San Francisco Chronicle for August 7, 1896. It appeared that Stetson, who was representing the Yosemite Valley Railway Company (Merced to El Portal, California. Abandoned 1945) had enlisted the aid of Thomas S. Bullock, a capitalist of Number 18 Wall Street, New York. Bullock, who was to furnish the rails for the Yosemite Valley RR from an old railroad of his in Arizona, at the last minute changed his mind and decided that he would build his own railroad in the Sierra country.

Whether or not this was the reason for Mr. Stetson's self destruction is not recorded. At any rate this choice bit of information was immediately copied by the local papers and the railroad rumors spread like wild fire. Strangely enough the prospect of better transportation was not looked upon as a boon to the mountain communities. In fact the subject became highly controversial and was good for either a lively argument or a fist fight at any time. There were almost as many opinions concerning the railroad as there were people in the county.

The editor of the Sonora "Democratic Banner" felt called upon to write a few remarks on that timely subject as follows:

"Eventually there will be heard the snort of the Iron Horse in this county, but we believe that the time is some distance away."

Regarding the economics involved ye editor continued to comment in a carefully worded manner no doubt designed to keep himself well outside of the shooting:

"Our opinion, after mature consideration, is that the benefit of a road into this country will be immense to certain channels of business and be an injury to others."

Hardly a Roger Babson yet his concluding sentence did contain a sage observation that was the crux of the entire situation. It was:

"However, when capitalists see that a road here will be a paying institution it will come."

As a whole the popular feeling was antagonistic toward the rails. People, apparently satisfied with their way of life, clung desperately to the creaking freight wagons and the bouncing stage coaches in the fear that mass transportation would demoralize local business and industry. The farmer, freighter, livery man and storekeeper saw only the ruination of their business and the "Union Democrat," apparently speaking for the majority, printed the following with feeling: "Sonora does not care for your railroad, gentlemen, keep your hands off." But in the next issue Mr. Bullock was quoted as saying: "I am certainly going to build a railroad into Tuolumne County," . . . and that was that.

If the people didn't want the railroad, there were large lumber interests that did; so Bullock stood ready to make good his threat. He was soon joined by Will H. Crocker and Crocker's royal brother-in-law Prince Ponaitowski who put the resources of their California Exploration Company behind the project.

On New Year's day 1897 the promoters arrived on the scene to look over the situation. During the month of January a survey was made and by February the property rights had been secured. March saw the beginning of grading at the Oakdale end of the line.

The West Coast Construction Company was to do most of the work with Cyrus Moreing of Stockton, a sub-contractor, handling the grading. But the skeptical residents didn't "set much store" by the coming of the railroad. Some predicted that the tracks would never get farther than 20 miles out of Oakdale, while many were convinced that this was just a spur of the Southern Pacific built to forestall competition.

By April 1897 the contractors were ready for rail and Mr. Bullock's men were busily engaged in pulling up his Prescott

& Arizona Central, which ran from Prescott to Seligman, Arizona until the Atlantic & Pacific ran parallel tracks forcing the little P. & A. C. out of business.

The steel was shipped from Arizona via the Santa Fe to Redondo Beach, California where it was loaded on coastal freighters and taken to Port Costa on upper San Francisco Bay. Here the material was again loaded on freight cars to resume the trip to Oakdale by rail. Ties and bridge lumber had already arrived on the scene and on April 2, 1897 the the first rail was laid on the Sierra Railway of California!

S. D. Freshman, who was the president of the road, announced now that everything was in readiness the line would be rushed through to completion. With these words the track laying was begun in earnest. It was even decided to put on another grading contractor. The new firm was Charles Erickson & Company, the people who did the work on the Santa Barbara division of the Southern Pacific at a reputed fee of $1,600,000 for sixteen miles. At any rate they were signed to do the heavy grading and rock work that was necessary in the higher mountains. For this purpose they were to put 300 head of horses and some 400 men on the job.

In the meantime two of the Sierra's engines had arrived in Oakdale and a third was in storage at Stockton. (One of these locomotives was the 3 spot, a 4-6-0, built as the Prescott & Arizona Central's No. 9. It ran on the Sierra until 1932 when it was taken out of service. Later it was reconditioned and used for motion picture work).

Yes, the railroad was on its way opposition not withstanding. However, the project must have acquired a certain amount of public acceptance because when the rails reached Coopertown, some 19 miles out of Oakdale, the Sonora stages made the rail head their western terminal and passengers and express were transferred to the train at that point.

But the rails didn't stop at Coopertown for long. Up the

sloping foothills of the Sierra they went until Jamestown was reached. "Jimtown", as it is called in the vernacular of the old timers, was an old town founded in 1848 during the height of the gold rush, but with the coming of the railroad a new town sprang up. The chief attraction and certainly the show place of the Sierra was the Hotel Nevills, an elaborate and spacious building built by Capt. W. A. Nevills, wealthy mining man who was one of the owners of the famous Rawhide Mine near Jamestown.

The hotel was built after the Oriental style of architecture with pointed, up-turned eaves and gables. It is interesting to note that many of the buildings and stations of the Sierra Railway were built along the same lines. Many people claim that it was the Hotel Nevills that set the theme. A great deal of sparkling quartz, taken from the various mines in the region went into the construction of the building and from its elevated site an excellent view was had of the old town beneath. The hotel itself acted as the railroad depot and passengers could step from the cars into the lobby where the best of service awaited. This mountain luxury hotel was operated by the railroad until it was destroyed by fire about 1915.

The Sierra Railway didn't rest at Jamestown for very long, because word soon came up that ex-congressman James A. Louttit had proposed a road from Stockton into the Sierra gold country with Sonora as their goal. In December of 1897 Louttit's company filed articles of incorporation to do business as the Stockton & Tuolumne Railroad.

The people of Sonora were delighted with the news. If they had to have a railroad, they would (for reasons of their own) rather have any railroad than the Sierra Railway. The Sierra, however, didn't lose any time building up to Sonora and the S. & T. never ran a train.

The people of Sonora were not the kind to hold a grudge,

however, and the first train to arrive in Sonora on the Sierra Railway touched off a great celebration. The Columbia and Sonora Coronet bands played for the event and the gay throng imbued with the spirit of the occasion seized the opportunity to commemorate the arrival of the railroad.

The same newspaper that had only a short time before printed the ". . . keep your hands off" story reversed its editorial policy enough ". . . to welcome the advent into the swellest mining town in the State that realized dream of many years . . . a locomotive and railway train".

By 1900 the rails had passed Sonora by almost thirteen miles and were entering the heavy timber region. The Frank Baker Ranch, which was the eastern terminal of the railroad, soon became the town of Tuolumne and the headquarters of the West Side Lumber Company. The lumber company laid about seventy miles of narrow gauge, known as the Hetch Hetchy & Yosemite Valley Railroad, back into some of the wildest country in the state.

About two miles west of Tuolumne is the little station of Ralph, named after F. J. Ralph, whose ranch was one of the show places of the county. Ralph is also the starting point of the Sugar Pine Railroad of the Pickering Lumber Company, which taps the vast belt of timber lying between the middle and south forks of the Stanislaus River. Close to 4,000 feet elevation, Ralph is the highest point on the Sierra Railroad and on a clear day one can see the fertile plains of the San Joaquin stretching westward toward the purple pinnacle of Mt. Diablo as part of an ever changing panorama fully appreciated by the trainmen on the Sierra.

In 1902 an eighteen mile branch line was completed from Jamestown to Angels Camp, the historic mining town where Mark Twain first heard the story of the "Jumping Frog" and Edwin Booth entertained the miners in the little theatre just off Raspberry Lane.

Photo by Jack R. Wagner

Photo by John P. Carrick

The Sierra Railroad at work.

The curves on the Angels branch were so sharp that extra short passenger cars were designed for that run. Photo shows mixed train on the Stanislaus River bridae.

Abandoned way station on the once busy Angels branch.

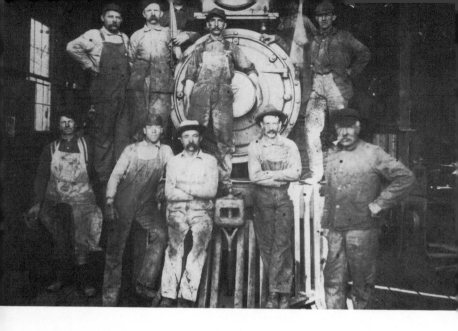

A bunch of the boys stop work long enough to have their picture taken. The locomotive is the No. 7 built in 1882 as Northern Pacific No. 93. After working on the Sierra for a time it was resold. Note the link and pin coupling.

An early inspection car.

Train time at Sonora. Above photo taken about 1915. Below, in the twenties.

From an old Post Card

The Angels branch was a picturesque little railroad serving the historic communities of Tuttletown, Melones (once one of the toughest mining towns in the state) and the mines of Carson Hill. It was at Carson Hill that one of the world's largest nuggets was found. It weighed 214 pounds troy and was valued at $44,000. Another bonanza was discovered at the fabulous Morgan Mine where $111,000 in gold was dislodged with a single blast.

The railroad to Angels Camp was something to behold with its 5% grade, three switchbacks and a lengthy span across the Stanislaus River. The curves were so sharp and the cuts so narrow (especially the Table Mountain cut near the Rawhide Mine) that special passenger equipment was used. One of these little cars, combination No. 5, is still being used as a caboose on the Sierra Railroad. These stubby coaches were actually not much longer than a conventional caboose and were usually pulled by an equally stubby locomotive of the Shay or Heisler type.

During its heyday the Angels branch performed a valuable freight and passenger service for an otherwise isolated section of the Mother Lode. A great deal of in and out freight from the mining activity supplied much of the revenue while the Columbia Marble Quarry shipped many carloads of their famous product over the Angels branch from Jefferson Spur. The local rock has been said to be equal in color and hardness to the finest Italian marble, and was much in demand. In San Francisco the Palace Hotel, Merchants Exchange, Standard Oil Building, Alaska and Rialto Buildings all used great quantities of Columbia marble that began its journey behind puffing Sierra locomotives.

The Angels branch seems to occupy a favorite spot in the memories of the residents and railroaders alike and judging by the stories that are told there never was a dull moment. Some of these tales are tragic while others are amusing, but added together they testify to a mighty dramatic eighteen miles of railroad.

Take the time, for instance, that engine No. 9 (a Heisler) was pulling its regular train over the branch, a train that contained a carload of dynamite. Now that in itself is not at all unusual for a train operating in a country of hard rock mines. The only feature that makes this particular trip a legend still told is that this time the car exploded. The engine and caboose stayed with the rails and the occupants remained safe, but the center section of the train, where the dynamite car was coupled, completely disintegrated taking with it two brakemen. The engineer, otherwise untouched, suffered the unnerving experience of having his cap torn by a passing piece of shrapnel. A set of car trucks landed at Jones' Mill, about a mile away, well ahead of the train that day and a cast steel car wheel can still be seen firmly imbedded in the bank an equal distance in the opposite direction. The scene of this mishap was known, even before the explosion, as Gee Whiz Point.

One of the most tragic of all accidents befell a passenger special carrying the Angels Camp baseball team. Near Tuttletown the passenger passed a work train which was engaged in switching an oil car for the Bell Mine. Everything seemed in order as the special passed, but the passenger train had descended only a mile or so of steep grade when the work train, completely out of control, speedily overtook it. Many of the passengers seeing the onrushing freight cars jumped out of the windows to save themselves. Two women were on the train, one with a tiny infant. In a moment of panic the mother threw the baby out of an open window and in a last desperate attempt to save themselves the women rushed for the platform only to be crushed at the moment of impact. The baby, caught on the fly, by an alert Angels Camp outfielder was the only member of his family to survive that tragic accident.

A happier story is found in the personality of Gus Swanson. Still an engineer on the Sierra Railroad, Gus was a veteran of the Angels branch. He is a good natured man and a fine engineer whose years of experience have made him an authoritative and respected roadbed critic. Now Gus's approach is by no means indirect. No, sir, Gus can always be depended on to do his part to remedy a bad situation. In the matter of the uneven roadbed Gus took to carrying wooden stakes in his cab and when he spied a poor section of track he would climb down from his slow moving Shay or Heisler, hammer a stake or two in the ground where John Azavedo, the section foreman, would be sure to see them and still have plenty of time to join his train.

That system worked fine with the little geared locomotives, but one day he was given No. 30, a powerful little rod engine, built especially for the Angels branch. Gus either underestimated the speed or the dimension of the new locomotive because when he climbed down to the bottom step to have a look along the rail he was surprised to find himself hanging by the seat of his pants on a cattle guard. Meanwhile the train with the firemen enjoying the ever lovely Sierra landscape went merrily on its way. Finally the tallow-pot, alarmed at the increasing speed, discovered he was alone in the cab and immediately stopped the train. Looking down the track he soon saw engineer Swanson, apparently none-the-worse for his experience, hot-footing it up the track in an honest effort to remount his iron horse.

It was on October 28, 1935, many years after the cattle guard episode that Gus Swanson and engine Number 30 pulled the last train out of Angels Camp, a train that took up and carried away the rails that neither would see again.

During its early history the Sierra Railway formulated some very ambitious plans for its future. One of these now forgotten schemes was known as the Yosemite Short Line.

This little subsidiary of the Sierra Railway was to run from Jamestown in a southeasterly direction into the Yosemite Valley. Prince Ponaitowski was highly enthusiastic and succeeded in raising much of the capital in France which necessitated the bonds being printed in both English and French.

Construction was begun on the 30-inch gauge Yosemite Short Line and the little rails soon spanned the distance between Jamestown and Jacksonville. The miniature locomotives were a sight to behold even if they didn't offer much in the way of pulling power. A flat car excursion was the first and last train over the road and that was the end of the Yosemite Short Line. Today most of the roadbed has succumbed to the ravages of the elements, but if you know just where to look you can still make out the old grade line as well as the remains of a couple of bridge piers that stand as the only monument to a lost cause.

Perhaps the most pretentious of all the Sierra Railway's contemplated projects was the proposed railroad over the summit of the rugged Sierra Nevada Mountains. This proposal called for—not a narrow gauge branch, but an extension of the standard gauge Sierra Railway itself!

In order to more fully appreciate the magnitude of this undertaking it should be remembered that at the time of this brazen idea only one railroad had ever attempted to cross the hump and the story of their struggle across the California-Nevada barrier is only too well known. Nevertheless the Sierra management was willing to attempt the feat—presumably with the intention of connecting with the Virginia & Truckee Railroad in Nevada to offer an alternate route for transcontinental traffic.

W. H. Newell, who was at that time chief engineer of the Sierra Railway, was commissioned to make the survey. Newell was familiar with the Central Pacific's hazardous route over Donner Pass where the highest stake driven marked an elevation of 7,042 feet, . . . where the snow remains well into June and the drifts measure from twelve to sixty feet deep and persist year after year. He had heard stories of how slides covered crew after crew and their frozen corpses were not to be found until the following spring when they were revealed still upright with their tools in their hands. Then there were the snow sheds—originally thirty-seven miles of them—built at a cost of anywhere from $10,000 to $30,000 a mile. Even after completion of the railroad there were operating costs and Newell realized only too well that the years of improvement and experience had not removed that thorn from the side of the Southern Pacific. So Engineer Newell carefully studied the problem from all angles and finally decided that the best method in the long run would be to tunnel!

His plans called for as easy a grade as possible to a point considerably lower than the Southern Pacific's snow bound seven thousand feet. At this point the proposed line would drive a four mile tunnel through the very heart of the mighty Sierra. The bore would not only reduce the climb, but at the same time would offer a snow-free right-of-way; a wise, but ambitious plan for a short line.

The survey was finished by April, 1906 and the complete report, together with papers ready for signatures were sent off to Prince Ponaitowski and his associates in France. By this time surely all of France must have heard of the Sierra Railway of California through the enthusiastic press agentry of his highness. Yes, the packet was mailed and postmarked April 17, 1906, the night before the great San Francisco earthquake! That disaster so upset financial circles that any additional expenditure was considered out of the question. Thus ended an ambitious attempt to cross the wild Sierra by rail and the great Sierra Tunnel . . . that might have been.

Meanwhile back at Jamestown at this same time and for this same reason there passed out of existence the afore-mentioned slim gauge Yosemite Short Line, which like so many native Californians never saw the towering cliffs of the state's most famous National Park.

The main line of the Sierra Railway continued to oper-ate, however, and during the boom period of irrigation and hydro-electric projects it played an important part. Material and machinery for at least three of California's great dams arrived on the job via the Sierra Railway. Perhaps the most famous was the Hetch Hetchy project of the City and County of San Francisco. From mile post 26 on the Sierra Railway, known as Hetch Hetchy Junction, there began a 56 mile mountain railroad to Mather. During the construction of the O'Shaughnessy Dam and other associated works of the Hetch Hetchy project trains were operated over this track-age by the Hetch Hetchy Railroad. A few years later, when it was decided to raise the level of the dam, arrangements were made for the Sierra Railway to use its power over the entire distance. In 1938 this practice was discontinued and the line reverted to the City of San Francisco. For a time it was oper-ated in connection with Hetch Hetchy maintenance with Plymouth gasoline locomotives supplying the motive power. The high costs of maintaining the line finally led to its aban-donment in 1938.

In 1922, when the Don Pedro Dam of the Turlock & Modesto Irrigation District was begun, a nine mile spur was laid from the Sierra main line over to the site on the Tuo-lumne River. And in 1923 a similar trackage was installed over to the Stanislaus River where the Melones Dam of the Oakdale and South San Joaquin Irrigation District was being constructed.

During this period of unusually heavy activity the Sierra Railway became one of the most profitable short lines in the country. Business became so brisk that two additional locomotives had to be rented from the Southern Pacific. The payroll listed 250 employes—with 14 engine crews alone!

As soon as the dams were completed, however, business returned to normal and in a few years it was to drop considerably less than normal. During the depression the lumber mills, usually the Sierra's most dependable source of revenue, closed down leaving the railroad with only a few weekly carloads of general merchandise. Finally on May 10, 1932 the company went into receivership and operated in that manner until March 31, 1937 when the property was put on the block at a foreclosure sale. A committee of former bondholders organized themselves and after turning in the successful bid took over the operation of the road. Thus the Sierra Railway of California became the Sierra Railroad Company, under which name and ownership it operates today.

On September 1, 1938 the new company discontinued passenger service by rail and began a bus service which they operated until they sold the franchise to the Greyhound Lines four years later.

At the present time the railroad company operates a fleet of trucks that run from Stockton to the mountain communities with mail, express and LCL deliveries leaving the rails for carload shipments only.

The present line of road runs from Oakdale at the edge of the San Joaquin Valley, through Jamestown and Sonora and into Tuolumne City, the eastern terminus—a total of 57 miles of railroad. The steepest grade is 3% and the greatest curvature is 18 degrees. Some 38 miles out of the 57 is curved track with 19 miles of tangent. Most of the road has been relaid with 90 lb. rail.

As this is written there are five steam locomotives in the roundhouse at Jamestown. However, on Sunday, April 17, 1955 the line officially changed over to Diesel operation. To cover the event a special train ran from Oakland and hundreds of rail fans and loyal friends of the Sierra Railroad paid a proper and reluctant farewell to the iron horse.

Although the faithful steam engines have been retired it's safe to say that W. C. Cheney, the Sierra's astute vice president and general manager will retain several for motion picture work because in addition to its regular service the Sierra Railroad is much in demand by the various motion picture companies. Whenever a script calls for special railroad effects you'll usually find that the producer has dispatched a location company to Jamestown. Don't think this is an imposition because the railroad people encourage the practice, keeping four wooden passenger coaches on hand just for this purpose. For this service the road has established a special tariff that covers just about anything that even Hollywood can think of doing.

Little No. 18, which was actually built in 1906, has been made up especially for the films with a diamond stack and gold leaf filigree to look like a real old timer. She has had more foreign roads painted on her tender than perhaps any other engine in the country. Here are just a few: In the picture "In Old Chicago" she was lettered C. & G.; for "Dodge City", she joined the A.T.&S.F.; "My Little Chickadee", Atlantic & Pacific Southern; "The Return of Frank James", St. Louis & Missouri; "When The Daltons Rode", Kansas, Missouri & Pacific; "Santa Fe Trail", Atchison & Topeka; "Bad Men of Wyoming", Missouri & Western; "Go West", New York & Western, and for "Duel In The Sun", the T. & S. W.

Gus Swanson, who is usually the engineer assigned to the movie trains remembers working on many pictures in addition to the ones mentioned. His list goes way back to some of the early Tom Mix thrillers. As a rule Gus likes working with picture people, although he says sometimes they don't know what they want.

But fireman Bill McCallum has his cue down pat. He knows what they want . . . it's smoke, lots of smoke . . . and good and black!

Photo by Al Rose

Sierra No. 34 pulling an excursion train past the Sonora station. August, 1937.

The historic depot at Sonora served as a utilitarian landmark. Note pointed gables.

From an old post card

When the Sonora depot burned in October, 1946, a proud old landmark was destroyed.

Not much information available on the above mishap.

Below: Three men were killed when this Heisler (No. 9) lost its air on a steep grade. The locomotive was rebuilt and later became No. 1 of the West Side Lumber Co.

Photos courtesy W. J. Tremewan

Roundhouse at Jamestown, 1937.

Coupon from Yosemite Short Line Bond. Because Prince Ponaitowski raised much of the capital in France the bonds were printed in both English and French.

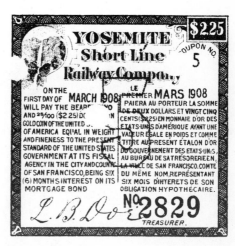

$2.25

YOSEMITE
Short Line
Railway Company

COUPON NO. 5

ON THE FIRST DAY OF MARCH 1908 WILL PAY THE BEARER NO AND 25/100 ($2.25) DO N GOLD COIN OF THE UNITED S OF AMERICA EQUAL IN WEIGHT AND FINENESS TO THE PRESENT STANDARD OF THE UNITED STATES GOVERNMENT AT ITS FISCAL AGENCY IN THE CITY AND COUNTY OF SAN FRANCISCO, BEING SIX (6) MONTHS INTEREST ON ITS MORTGAGE BOND

LE PREMIER MARS 1908 PAIERA AU PORTEUR LA SOMME DE DEUX DOLLARS ET VINGT CINQ CENTS ($2.25) EN MONNAIE D'OR DES ETATS-UNIS D'AMÉRIQUE AYANT UNE VALEUR ÉGALE EN POIDS ET COMME TITRE AU PRESENT ÉTALON D'OR DU GOUVERNEMENT DES ETATS-UNIS AU BUREAU DE SA TRÉSORERIE EN, LA VILLE DE SAN FRANCISCO. COMTE DU MÊME NOM, REPRÉSENTANT SIX MOIS D'INTERETS DE SON OBLIGATION HYPOTHÉCAIRE.

L. B. Do NO 2829
TREASURER.

Engine No. 36 stops for a drink near Warnerville

Compound No. 28 heads east into the Sierra country. Photo taken
March 1955.

Extra west with Sierra 18 nearing the Summit at Ralph, highest point on the Sierra Railroad. February, 1949.

Extra west with No. 36 near the same location. February, 1955.

Photos by Jack R. Wagner

Train time at Tuolumne.

At Tuolumne engineer Gus Swanson climbs down to oil the crosshead.

Bill McCallum, the smiling fireman of the Sierra Railroad.

Photos by Jack R. Wagner

The Hetch Hetchy Railroad was a major piece of construction. It began at a connection with the Sierra Railroad at Hetch Hetchy Junction, 26 miles from Oakdale, and extended for 68 miles to the rim of Hetch Hetchy Valley. It was built for the construction of the Hetch Hetchy project and was operated as a common carrier by the City and County of San Francisco from 1918 to 1925.

Above: H. H. R. R. shops at Groveland (May 10,1919)
Below: Hetch Hetchy train at Rattlesnake. (May 10, 1919)

Photos courtesy Hetch Hetchy Water Supply

The H.H. R.R. was built at a cost of approximately $3,000,000.
During peak operations the City operated six owned and one
rented locomotives. Upon completion of the O'Shaughnessy Dam
and associated works most of the rolling stock was sold. The track
was then maintained only for light gasoline locomotives used for
maintenance of equipment. Later the 9 miles from Mather to the
dam were removed.

Above: Hetch Hetchy R.R. shops at Groveland looking south. (1918)

Below: H.H. R.R. at dam site. Large well dressed man in truck is
City Engineer M. M. O'Shaugnessy.

Photo courtesy Hetch Hetchy Water Supply

In 1934 the remaining 59 mile length of the H.H. R.R. was restored to proper condition for the heavy hauling necessary for the enlargement of the O'Shaugnessy Dam and was operated under contract by the Sierra Railroad until that work was completed in 1938. The H.H. R.R. was abandoned shortly afterward.

Above: Hetch Hetchy Railroad No. 3 (May 10, 1919)

Below: Sierra Railroad No. 34 at Mather during the time the H.H. R.R. was operated as a branch of the Sierra.

Photo by Al Rose

TECRASILK PHOTO

A real old timer. Built by Rogers in 1891 she was brought to the Sierra Railroad during the construction days. Retired in 1932, but retained for motion picture work.

Lima Shay built in 1903. Sold to the Pickering Lumber Co. in 1924.

Photo courtesy Sierra Railroad

No. 18 Baldwin 1906. Retired 1953.

No. 22. Equipped with snow plow for use on Hetch Hetchy R.R.
Baldwin 1920. Sold to California Western 1940. Scrapped.

No. 24. Ex Nevada Copper Belt R.R. No. 3. Scrapped 1955.

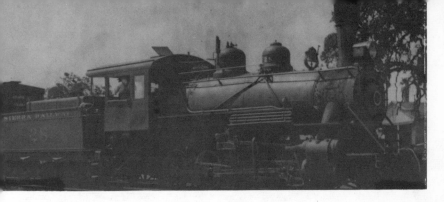

No. 28 was built by Baldwin in 1922.

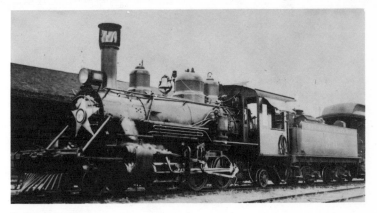

No.30. Veteran of the Angels branch and the pride of engineer Gus Swanson.

One car train on the Angels branch. Locomotive No. 32 was sold to Tidewater Southern. Ended up as stationary boiler at a mine in Nevada.

No. 36 was built for the Sierra Railroad in 1930.

A locomotive in grease paint. No. 18 made up for the films plays
the part of an early engine on the Atchison, Topeka & Santa Fe

Made up for the movies with diamond stack and gold leaf filigree, little No. 18 has seen more foreign roads painted on her tender than any other engine in the country.

No. 18 takes a spill! Actually it is a carefully arranged double.
Used in the filming of "Duel In The Sun"

Steam fans went wild when the Sierra R.R. purchased this huge compound in 1952 . . . and were equally sad when the road went Diesel in 1955.

Photo by John P. Carrick

CHAPTER VI

THE ELY ROUTE

EVER SINCE THE DAYS of the fabulous bonanza mines Nevada has been used to the feverish waves of prosperity that would overnight transform a lonely mining camp of tents and shacks into a hustling desert city. These recurring cycles of wild excitement and the scramble for newly discovered riches became virtually a continual process and as soon as one camp began to decline others came into existence to feed the tension of the times and to nourish the economy of the state.

During the earlier days men visualized only gold and silver and the less spectacular ores, which occurred more frequently, were ignored in the mad stampede for the more precious metals. This condition changed, however, when Thomas Edison, the Wizard of New Jersey, startled the world with his "crazy" ideas and inventions. So it was when electricity shocked people and industry out of their lethargy and ushered in a new era there grew a great demand for lead, zinc and greatest of all . . . copper! Fortunately this came about at a time when the great gold and silver deposits were either exhausted or failing and the mining world turned to the production of ores formerly disregarded.

The mining history of the "sagebrush state" can roughly be divided into the following periods: (1) the Comstock Lode; (2) Tonapah silver; (3) Jewelry-ore at Goldfield, and (4) the decline of the gold and silver towns and the increased demand for copper. And, so, as the copper age descended on Nevada there began, once again, the familiar cycle of mining camps and towns rising and falling on the precarious tides of fortune. Out of this period of the state's history, however, there developed the concentrated little copper cummunity of Ely, now key city of eastern Nevada.

Nestled in a canyon of the Egan Range, Ely has assumed a somewhat metropolitan aspect as well as an air of permanence and stability unusual for a mining town. And, today, even after fifty years of almost continuous operation it is said that the mines are assured of a copper supply that will last another fifty years. So as long as the price and the supply hold up Ely will retain the title of Nevada's leading mining boomtown. (The residents of Ely insist that their town isn't entirely dependent upon copper as its sole support. They point out stockraising, poultry producing, dairying and general commerce.)

The first discovery of valuable mineral in this section of Nevada was reported by employes of the old Overland Stage Company in 1859 although reports are somewhat vague as to just what this "mineral" was. Gold, however, was later discovered in the Egan Canyon by soldiers from Fort Shellbourne under Captain Tober in 1863 and the first mill for treating ore was erected on the site the following year.

In 1867 a character, history informally refers to merely as "Indian John", had guided a party of prospectors to what he believed to be a likely spot and the following year brought results. A ten ton blast furnace was built to serve the district in 1869 and the next year a 10-stamp mill began operations. Production was disappointing and neither these mills nor those erected in later years returned much of a profit.

It wasn't until 1886 that the little community began to get some publicity. This was the year that the county seat was moved from the declining gold mining town of Hamilton and established in what is now Ely. The next three years saw an increase in prestige and the addition of another stamp mill or two, but nothing other than this occurred that would be apt to make the headlines of history, although it was about this time that the town acquired its present name of ELY. This came about, it seems, when one A. J. Underhill borrowed $5,000 from John Ely of Pioche for the purpose of buying and developing the townsite and, either out of gratitude or shrewdness, the real estate operator named his project after his benefactor.

Ely, the man, was a typical western mining promoter who had come to Pioche from Montana. His chief claim to notoriety at that time was, as rumor had it, that he had been an associate of Jack Slade. Mr. Slade was a former superintendent in the Julesburg section for the Overland Stage Company and was dismissed because of an uncontrollable temper when drunk. His inability to win friends and influence people is further shown by the fact that he was eventually hanged by Montana vigilantes for "dangerous and unwise use of firearms".

Mr. Ely, who made the news himself on occasion, once paid $3,500 for a mine which he turned around and sold for almost a third of a million. On the surface this might look like good business, but the last laugh was on brother Ely as the mine produced some $20,000,000 for the new owners.

Not a man to be bitter, Ely lived in fine style on his $300,000 and it was while looking for better ways to spend his money that he went to Paris. But, happiness was not to be his in the French capitol and he soon lost both his money and his wife. For a while he tried to drown his sorrows in whisky, but he eventually recovered and was able to make and lose several fortunes before he died. Truly a colorful figure of the West was John Ely.

Ely, the town, continued as a colorful western mining camp. The big strike was yet to come.

It was summer in 1900 when two young men arrived in town to work in the mines. They were Dave Bartley and Edwin Gray of Shasta County, California. Prospectors at heart they decided to look around a little on their own before hiring themselves out as laborers. One of the claims that came to their attention was the "Ruth" which was owned by D. C. McDonald, the local justice of the peace and was named for his daughter. With the prospector's zest for the unknown the two newcomers took a lease with an option to buy the "Ruth" and one other claim for $3,500. Bartley, who had some experience with copper ore, believed their new holdings contained this metal.

With their money invested in the property the two men had little left to eat on so W. B. Graham, the owner of Ely's general store agreed to grubstake the miners. There followed two years of hard work and during that time the men slowly drove a 300 foot tunnel at the end of which they sunk a 200 foot shaft. Their work was rewarded with ore, and just as Bartley had suspected—copper ore! What's more, as they progressed, the ore body became richer.

Bartley and Gray's prospects for the future might have looked bright but for one thing; the "Ruth" was situated in an isolated area some 150 miles south of the Central Pacific (Southern Pacific) and 85 miles and three mountain ranges east of the Eureka & Palisades Railroad. Gold and silver ores may be reduced to bullion with comparative ease and the valuable bars carried out on mule back if necessary, but copper ore, producing from 10 to 20 pounds to the ton requires considerable equipment for smelting and even when the ore has been reduced to its metallic content the copper matte is extremely bulky and therefore costly to ship to market.

For a time the problem of transportation remained the chief fly in the ointment and the mining world passed over this new discovery as too costly an operation. Eventually, however, the enthusiasm of Bartley and Gray attracted Joe Bray of Austin, Nevada. Mr. Gray was favorably impressed and immediately organized a company to develop the "Copper Flat" claims a mile to the east of the "Ruth."

There wanders into the story at this time an inquisitive prospector, who in the guise of an old Comestocker obtains information on the new mines. It was his favorable report that attracted Mark L. Requa, the manager of the Eureka & Palisades Railroad. Requa went straight to Bartley and Gray and asked them to name their price for an option. Their reply was "$150,000" and the deal was closed at once. (At this writing Dave Bartley was retired and living at Carson City, Nevada. Ed Gray, after selling his share of the "Ruth," made another lucky strike at Contact, Nevada. Later it was through Gray's influence that the Union Pacific built the Twin Falls to Wells branch.).

It had been Requa's idea to extend the Eureka & Palisades over the 85 miles that separated Eureka and Ely and into the promising new copper country. His first step was to organize the White Pine Copper Company. When an unexpected opportunity arose to acquire the "Copper Flat" holdings also, he found it was necessary to obtain further financial help. So with the bolstering effect of eastern money the final result was that all holdings were merged late in 1904 in a move which produced the Nevada Consolidated Copper Company with Requa as vice-president and general manager.

By this time it was decided that the extension of the narrow gauge Eureka & Palisades Railroad would be too expensive, so it was proposed that the copper interests build their own line into Ely from the north. And so it was for this purpose that the Nevada Northern Railway Company was incorporated on May 29, 1905 and construction was begun shortly thereafter.

The contract for building the road was awarded to the Utah Construction Company, the contracting firm that later became one of the Six Companies of Hoover Dam fame. Headquarters during construction was established at Cobre on the main line of the Southern Pacific some 140 miles north of Ely.

It is said that during this period of heavy construction in the Ely district it was difficult to obtain shipments of machinery and materials. The reason has been given that San Francisco at the time was busily engaged in rebuilding its earthquake and fire destroyed city thereby causing a shortage of materials and a transportation snarl reminiscent of wartime conditions. Stories are told of expediters being sent to shipping points and railroad yards with pockets bulging with five dollar bills which they used to advantage.

The line of road extends across a portion of the "Great American Desert" and was not a very difficult piece of construction. In fact the country traversed is so flat that the grade never exceeds one per cent and in the entire 140 miles of main line there is neither a tunnel nor trestle—nothing but track and sagebrush from Cobre to East Ely.

With such a gradient the power required is not usually large, but on occasion this didn't seem to prove out. When the Cole Brothers' Circus was due to play Ely locomotive #20 was sent out to bring the show train in from the junction. When the engine crew tied on they soon discovered that their locomotive was insufficient to move the huge railroad show regardless of level track. Consequently they had to wire for additional power. As the result of the delay there was no circus parade in Ely that day, although the show did go on as per schedule and tradition.

It was during the days of construction of the railroad and the opening of the mines that East Ely came into being. The East Ely townsite company was formed for the purpose of creating a town for the employes of the mining and smelting companies. This plan didn't sit well with the residents of the original Ely as they could see no reason why their already established town, only a mile away, should be ignored. The promoters of the townsite company were smart operators, however, and had managed to tie up most of the available property in Ely with options thereby forcing any interested newcomer over to East Ely where real estate was available—for a price.

Trouble developed when the new Ely attempted to tap the same spring that supplied water to the old Ely. The indignant Elyites camped on their hillside armed with shotguns to prevent the construction of a pipeline.

In spite of many difficulties the prospects of the little town of East Ely were for a time quite good. But the depression of 1907 retarded its development to such an extent that when technical employes arrived to work in the new copper industry they were forced to settle around their respective plants. This condition led to the establishment of McGill as the smelter town and Ruth and Kimberly as the mining communities. The mine and smelter towns are about twenty miles apart with Ely and its little suburb, East Ely about half way between them.

Today East Ely remains as the headquarters for the Nevada Northern and here one finds the general offices, roundhouse and car shops. In the southern end of the railroad yard there still stands a tall stack beside a large windowless building. This was intended by the East Ely developers to be the power house, but the plant was never completed and the community along with the others obtains its electricity from the central plant at McGill.

The Nevada Northern Railway was organized, built and equipped in a little over a year. It reached Ely in September of 1906 and the twenty-ninth of the month was set aside by the local people as "Railroad Day" and there resulted a celebration that is remembered and talked about in Ely to this day. Three special trains converged on the Nevada Northern at Cobre, from Salt Lake City, Ogden and Reno. Many celebrities of the day arrived including the energetic Tex Rickard, who was always looking for excitement and opportunity. Locomotives and stations were decorated with wreaths of native sagebrush and, as the first Nevada Northern special headed toward Ely, the day became a Mardi Gras.

In the beginning there was some agitation to build a smelter near Ely, but an agreement was finally reached and it was decided to build the huge plant at the McGill site. Work was commenced in 1907 and the first ore was reduced a year later.

The large scale open cut mining operations were begun also in 1907 with the removal of the overburden. Actual ore production at Copper Flat began in 1908. By that time a rail line had been built from the mine to the mill, about 23 miles. This road, actually a part of the Nevada Northern, is operated as a branch line.

As might be expected, continuous digging in one spot for almost fifty years has resulted in quite a sizeable hole in the ground. As a matter of fact the pit at Copper Flat is considered to be one of the largest man-made holes in the world. It measures a mile long, ⅝ of a mile wide and has an average depth of over 500 feet. To date, the Kennecott Copper Corporation has removed 120,954,000 tons of ore and 179,-132,865 tons of waste. This has produced 2,490,000,000 pounds of copper valued at $387,690,000, as well as 1,255,573 ounces of gold and 3,488,300 ounces of silver with a total valuation of $39,304,795.

The actual earth moving is accomplished by six huge electric shovels weighing 165 tons apiece and capable of scooping up 10 tons of earth and rock at a single bite. These shovels deposit the material in standard gauge railway cars that make their way in and out of the pit by means of some 14 miles of track. The track is frequently shifted to provide access to the ore and at no point does the grade exceed two per cent.

The ore cars hold 75 tons and it formerly required two of the little 85 ton tank locomotives for each eight cars. Today Diesel-electric locomotives are used in the pit entirely and one large Diesel now hauls an eight car train, a total of 600 tons per train. Smaller Diesels in the pit are used for spotting cars at the shovels.

The Kennecott Copper Corporation is also processing ore, or will in the near future, from other locations including the Kimberly Pit, started in 1952; The Veteran Pit, begun in October, 1953; and the Deep Ruth Shaft, expected to be in production late in 1955.

The result of all this mining activity is taken to the staging area where it is made up into 30 car trains for the trip to the smelter. Once the work of big coal-burning consolidations with paradoxically shrill whistles, now Diesel locomotives have come to the "Ore Line."

K. C. C. ore delivery trains operating over Nevada Northern tracks are now scheduled for 10 trains of 30 loads and 10 trains of empties daily, or 300 loads a day seven days a week.

Originally the Nevada Northern did the actual hauling of ore from Ruth to McGill on a tariff basis, but since about 1920 the copper company has operated the trains on a trackage agreement. Under this arrangement the locomotives are owned by the mining interests and are operated by their employes, but they run under Nevada Northern supervision and the equipment is maintained at the railroad's shops at East Ely. Of course, actually the Nevada Northern is controlled by the copper company, but they prefer to operate the railroad as a separate enterprise.

TECRASILK PHOTO

The Nevada Northern's high wheeled No. 40 and two car train at Ely station ready for the 139 mile run to Cobre. (1934)

COPPER PIT - RUTH, NEV.

APPROXIMATE SIZE-
1 MILE LONG - ⅝ MILE WIDE - 700 Ft.
13 LEVELS
OUTPUT 75,000,000. TONS MILLING

Copper Pit at Ruth, Nevada. One of the largest man-made holes in the world it measures a mile long, ⅝ of a mile wide and has an average depth of over 500 feet. To date, the Kennecott Copper Corp. has removed 120,954,000 tons of ore and 179,132,865 tons of waste. This has produced 2,490,000,000 pounds of copper valued at $387,690,000 as well as 1,255,573 ounces of gold and 3,488,300 ounces of silver with a total valuation of $39,304,795.

"COPPER PIT" RUTH NEV.

Ruth, Nevada. Below, railroad station at Ruth. Note the 502, one of the steam locomotives used in the Pit at that time.

Photo by Jack R. Wagner

The Consolidated Copper Corp. operates deep mines at Kimberly.

Little used R.R. station at Kimberly.

Photo by Jack R. Wagner

Differing from the main line out to Cobre, which is laid with 60 pound rail across the level desert, the "Ore Line" branch of the Nevada Northern is gravel ballasted with 90 pound rail and will soon be relaid with 110 pound. Also, the 23 mile stretch through the Egan Canyon up to the mines was not so simple a construction job. Originally the line had two tunnels, but some years ago one was cut through.

There is a noticeable grade on this section of railroad, but fortunately the only work required against the grade is with the returning empty ore cars. Of course the trip down from the mines with a typical load of around 3,000 tons requires that the train be kept under absolute control.

The story is told of a runaway ore train that came down the mountain strictly on its own. Thundering along the track that skirts Ely it miraculously streaked through the East Ely yard traffic at an estimated 80 miles an hour. Once clear of the yard the train began the "up" grade to McGill and its energy was soon arrested. Although this presents a hair raising picture fortunately the incident was not tragic and can be put down as a close call that today makes a good railroad yarn.

As a matter of fact that runaway story was about the best thriller we were able to dig up on the Nevada Northern. And while it may not liven up these pages it certainly speaks well of the excellent safety record of the railroad.

Oh, they have their derailments—what railroad doesn't go on the ground now and then—but the point is they haven't had what might be called a serious derailment or wreck and to date there have been no fatalities resulting from such an accident. Consequently in a shed at East Ely you can see a huge 100 ton railway crane—a beautiful piece of machinery—that only sees the road once in the proverbial coon's age. More than just good luck it would seem that a great deal of credit for this excellent safety record should go to the management's intelligent and ever active campaign of "safety first" on the Nevada Northern.

In all fairness to facts, however, we must record the one passenger wreck on the road. This was back in 1919 when a main line passenger collided with a school train. No serious injuries resulted.

With the mention of the school train an interesting service is recalled. Before the days of school buses the Nevada Northern operated morning and evening commute specials for the students of the community. Two trains were used in this service, one starting from McGill and the other from Kimberly and Ruth up on the hill. These trains brought the youngsters from the outlying districts to the high school at Ely. When school buses came into vogue the trains were removed from service and the cars were sent up to the pit where they became "shift cars" and transported the men in and out of the workings.

During the passenger carrying days the Nevada Northern was an extremely busy road. The coach fare from Ely to Cobre in those days was $10 and a time card issued in 1909 shows 44 regularly scheduled trains. Of course, many of these were in what was called "Ping-Pong" service. This was a shuttle system operated between Ely and East Ely. The distance is only one mile, but the little interurban provided a useful means of traversing the then muddy streets. Also of interest to time table collectors is the fact that this same 1909 issue shows the Nevada Northern operating on "Mountain Time." This, we are told, is reminiscent of the days when the Southern Pacific ran on M.T. as far west as Sparks, Nevada and the Nevada Northern, connecting with the S. P., found it expedient to use their kind of time.

These were also the days of overnight Pullman service between Ely and Salt Lake City and a twice a week Pullman run to Oakland, California. But the snappy Pullman trains eventually degenerated into a baggage car and two coaches, then to a baggage car and one coach and finally on August 1, 1941 passenger service by rail was dropped entirely.

It was then that the railroad turned to the highway for its mail and passenger business. Two G.M.C. buses, the last word in highway transportation, are operated by the company, making one round trip daily between Ely and Wells, Nevada. These buses were designed especially for the Nevada Northern and contain many unusual features. Their interior appointments even includes a completely equipped rest room—highly desirable as stops are infrequent on the long desert run.

In the early days of the railroad and especially during the years 1916, '17 and '18 business was exceptionally good. The old records show a gross passenger revenue of $125,000 a year while the freight business reached $2,000,000. It was during this first flush of enthusiasm that there were rumors of building on, connecting with other railroads and such. One project, that was discussed almost before the road had reached Ely, was the Tonopah extension. Fired by the excitement of the Tonopah discovery and the usual difficulties of freighting into a new territory, certain people suggested a continuation of the Ely Route into Tonopah, but that plan was considered inadvisable and died a natural death when the Tonopah & Goldfield Railroad came into the picture.

There was also some talk of connecting the Nevada Northern with the San Pedro, Los Angeles & Salt Lake Railroad (later acquired by the Union Pacific) at Pioche some 100 miles south of Ely. Although this extension might have given the Union Pacific a useful north south line in Nevada nothing ever came of it.

In 1910 the Nevada Consolidated, which was largely controlled by Guggenheim's Utah Copper Company, absorbed the Cumberland-Ely interests. The mines, mills railroad and other properties of the companies continued to operate under the name Nevada Consolidated until 1943. At that time the Nevada Consolidated Copper Company was acquired by the Kennecott Copper Company, although as far as actual operation was concerned this change of ownership meant little more than a new letterhead and the Nevada Northern didn't even get that.

Today two round trips a week between East Ely and the S. P. main line at Cobre with the road's new (1952) 1500 H.P. EMD Diesel-electric Road Switcher provides all of the freight service necessary. Some of this traffic is, of course, general merchandise for the commerce of the community and during the spring and fall seasons there is a great deal of live-stock shipping. But regardless the copper company is still the main reason for the railroad and about 90% of the road's business is with the parent company. Inbound fuel, machinery and materials and outbound blister copper weighing 400 pounds a bar make up most of the main line tonnage.

The busy "Ore Line" doesn't take a back seat to anybody's railroad. In fact during one typical period (1940 to 1944) this section of the Nevada Northern averaged 12 million ton miles per month. An interesting figure even when compared with some of the country's trunk lines. (Although we won't vouch for its accuracy someone once figured that the ton-miles of this 23 mile stretch of track exceeds that of the New York Central.)

While the Nevada Northern does not use steam locomotives any more, they have on hand at East Ely three veteran coal-burners. There is passenger No. 40, built in 1910, a trim, high stepping 4-6-0 with huge 62″ drivers; freight No. 81, a 2-8-0 built in 1917 and little K.C.C. tank locomotive No. 93, a veteran of the Pit since 1909. All others have been scrapped.

The Nevada Northern's record of safety and efficiency is to a great extent attributable to the efforts and abilities of its management. For a number of years, for instance, Mr. H. J. Beem was vice-president and general manager of the road. Mr. Beem had seen a variety of railroad operations before his connection with the Nevada Northern and had ample opportunity to prove his ideas of good management. Originally an Illinois Central man he came west to join the Western

Pacific as division superintendent, a position he held in Elko, Nevada and Sacramento, California for some 26 years.

During Mr. Beem's regime H. A. Fravel was superintendent of the road. Fravel likewise brought a good many years of railroading to the copper pike, beginning his career with the Chicago, Burlington & Quincy. He joined the Southern Pacific in 1907 where he was employed, except for two slack periods during which he hired out to the historic Virginia & Truckee, until he came to East Ely.

At the close of 1951 both Mr. Beem and Mr. Fravel retired and Mr. H. M. Peterson, who had been associated with H. J. Beem on the Western Pacific and later worked for him on the Nevada Northern as trainmaster, was promoted to the newly created position of general superintendent. Since that time the actual operation of the system has been in his hands.

There are many other competent executives and railroaders on the Nevada Northern and it is regrettable that personal mention can not be made of them all, because to them and their predecessors goes the honor and distinction of transforming a drab, desert mining camp into a busy, prosperous city. Perhaps no other group contributed quite so much to the economy and ultimate destiny of the Ely district of Nevada.

Without transportation there could be no commerce.

The actual earth moving is accomplished by huge electric shovels weighing 165 tons and capable of scooping up 10 tons of earth and rock at a single bite.

Photo by Chas. D. Gallagher

The shovels deposit the material in 75 ton capacity railway cars which make their way in and out of the pit by means of some 14 miles of track.

Photo by Chas. D. Gallagher

A 30 car ore train in the Egan Canyon on the 23 mile run to the smelter at McGill.

Main business section, Ely, Nevada.

Formerly the Nevada Northern station at Ely the building is now owned by the Railway Express Company.

Photo by Jack R. Wagner

Nevada Con. Mill — McGill Nev.
943

Mill at McGill, Nevada

Nevada Northern Station at McGill

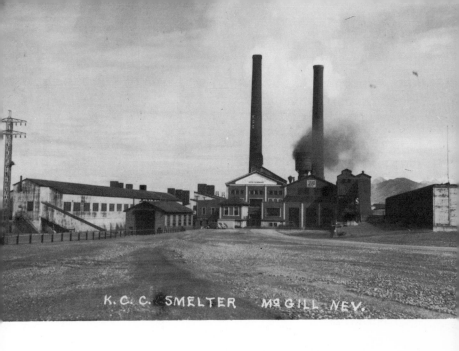

K. C. C. SMELTER   McGILL NEV.

Kennecott Copper Corp. smelter at McGill, Nevada

Diesel-electric switchers are used in the smelter yard at McGill.

Photo by Jack R. Wagner

The "R. E. Noble", the Nevada Northern's colorful high-wheel passenger engine once went 377,000 miles before her wheels were dropped or her tires changed. Today she rests in the car shop at East Ely painted and shiny, a masterpiece of the locomotive builder's art.

Passenger equipment formerly used on the N.N. Color: Green. Photo taken July, 1938.

No. 11 (originally No. 7) was built by American in 1907.

Once the Nevada Northern boasted a Railway Post Office.

Originally built as a saddle tank (No. 5) for American Smelting this 2-8-0 was rebuilt as Nevada Northern No. 80.

This steel "commuter" coach was used before the days of school buses to transport school children. It became a "shift" car and carried men down in the pit. Color: green. (Photo taken 1939)

Prior to the coming of the Diesel most of the work on the Nevada Northern was done by the No. 81, the only steam locomotive on the road equipped with a mechanical stoker.

Nevada Northern passenger coach used before this service went to the highway.

Photos by Jack R. Wagner

An outfit car at East Ely stands ready to roll with the "big hook". Typical Nevada Northern freight car.

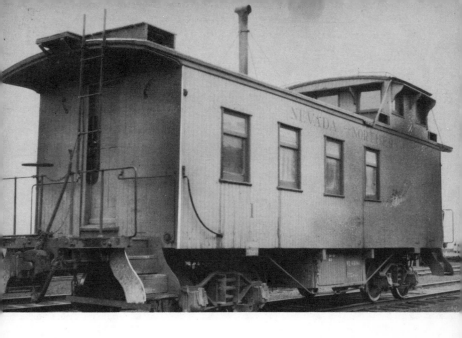

Painted a bright yellow this is a typical Nevada Northern caboose used on main line freight. The four wheel job below is used by Kennecott on the "ore line". Color also yellow.

Photo by Jack R. Wagner

Round house at East Ely, Nevada

Photo by Jack R. Wagner

No longer needed in the days of Diesel the coal bunker and stock pile was once a highly necessary operation.

Photos by Jack R. Wagner

General office of the Nevada Northern Railway Company at East Ely, Nevada.

Safety first is both the trade mark and watch word of The Ely Route.

Photo courtesy Nevada Northern Railway

In 1952 this 1500 h.p. Diesel-electric was put into main line service and the age of steam came to an end on the Nevada Northern.

CHAPTER VII

THE END OF THE N.C.B.

IT WAS IN DECEMBER OF 1946 when I went to San Francisco to see the officials of the Nevada Copper Belt Railway Company. The general offices were in the Fife Building on Drumm Street, a strange combination of nomenclature that at one time managed to get into Ripley's "Believe It or Not" columns and is considered by many San Franciscans as a close runner-up to their other famous number, "1 Polk and 2 Fell." However, there is nothing at all unusual about the building itself and the more sedate occupants, not wishing to have levity on their letterheads, refer to it as merely "Number One Drumm Street."

Stepping from the elevator at the eighth floor I entered the offices of the Parr Richmond Terminal Company, the parent company of the Nevada Copper Belt Railway. Mr. T. A. Goodrick, according to the Official Railway Guide, was the vice-president and traffic manager, so in due time I was introducing myself to him. He seemed a little surprised to learn that I was interested in writing the story of the N.C.B.

"That's funny," he said, "nearly everyone who comes up to see us regarding the Copper Belt these days is a junk man." "You see," he continued, "we have applied for abandonment."

I told him that I wasn't aware of that, but if such was the case it would be all the more valuable for story material as their difficulties were, no doubt, all too typical of short line troubles in general. Mr. Goodrick sighed a little.

"Yes, these are the days railroads are sold by the ton and not by the mile."

Then as he leaned back in his leather desk chair he recalled his younger days as a railroader and it wasn't too difficult to see that the lure of the rails still held its charm.

I also met Mr. Fred D. Parr, the president and Mr. Fred Cox, the young secretary and general manager of the railroad. Both heartily endorsed my little project and seemed anxious to have their railroad appear in print even if it wasn't much of a money maker.

Some time later, with the company's blessing and complete cooperation, I set out for Nevada to meet the dramatis personae and to actually witness the "end of the N.C.B."

This short line, which in recent years had been pruned down to the 28 miles between Wabuska and Hudson, was once a lively railroad closely tied to the mining activity of the area. In fact the road was built because of the demands of the Nevada-Douglas Consolidated Copper Company which at that time was investing a great deal of money in their property at Ludwig. This development, together with the Blue Stone and the Mason Valley Mines, provided ample reason for a railroad and during the lush days also provided more than ample revenue.

Possibly it was by pre-arrangement that the Nevada-Douglas people built the railroad and the Mason Valley Mining Company constructed the smelter, anyway this led to a working agreement between the two companies which was apparently successful and for many years the ore trains from

Ludwig and Mason made regular and frequent trips to the furnaces at Thompson.

But, let's begin at the beginning. On March 17, 1909 at Salt Lake City, Utah, the board of directors of the Nevada-Douglas Consolidated Copper Company aproved of an agreement entered into by vice-president A. J. Orem and secretary W. C. Orem (brothers) with J. G. Jacobs and others to begin, at once, the survey for a proposed railway line from the Nevada-Douglas Copper Company mines at Ludwig to the Southern Pacific Lines to the north. Five days later, on March 22, the Nevada Copper Belt Railroad Company was incorporated under the laws of the state of Maine.

During the summer months preliminary surveys had been made and a right-of-way was secured over what was considered the most desirable route. In a contract dated November 15, 1909 the Nevada Copper Belt Railroad Company authorized the Mason & Douglas Construction Company to build and equip the railroad. This Mason & Douglas Company was presumably organized for the express purpose of building the road since its date of incorporation was scarcely a month prior to the awarding of the contract. Regardless of that active construction work was instituted immediately out of Wabuska, a point on the Southern Pacific's line (formerly the Carson & Colorado RR) from Hazen to Tonopah Junction.

By January 14th of 1910 the N.C.B. had been completed to Yerington, Nevada, a distance of 11.5 miles. Mason was reached a month later and on March 1st that part of the road from Wabuska to Mason was formally turned over to the Nevada Copper Belt Railroad Company for operation.

The summer months of 1910 saw little progress made past Mason due to the grading contractors not having their work sufficiently ahead to permit track laying at an advantage. For the next few months Mason remained the southern terminus of the N.C.B. and even after the road built on, this town remained an important stop. Since the advent of the Blue Stone and the Mason Valley Mines in the hills above town, Mason had grown into quite a little city having a commodious hotel, a modern school (built at a cost of $15,000), church, bank, theatre, drug store, mercantile houses of various sorts, steam laundry, public recreation grounds, a newspaper, fully equipped hospital and, according to a promotional bulletin issued at the time, "other legitimate enterprises." No doubt there were also enterprises not so legitimate, but, then again, that's only heresay.

The Blue Stone mine was situated on a hill high above Mason and from the mine to the N.C.B. a little Heisler locomotive tugged its long strings of empties up the steep grade and did its best to hold back the loaded ore cars on the way down. Sometimes the tonnage was too much and the engineer would lose control of his train. The crew, having no intention of riding down that hill under such conditions, would unload leaving the Heisler to do what it could. Many times the little locomotive would streak into Mason completely deserted. Fortunately there was a slight rise nearby and the locomotive would either die completely or slow down to the point where someone from the N.C.B. could board her and shut her down. P. H. Cook, who for many years was superintendent of the Nevada Copper Belt, is said to have left his offiice on occasion to climb aboard the abandoned Heisler.

Active construction work was resumed in September, 1910 between Mason and Hudson. The going was slow, however, and the next 15 miles required a period of six months. This was due to the difficulties encountered in the Walker River Canyon where considerable cutting, filling and additional engineering was made necessary because of the narrow canyon and the contour of the winding river. Hudson, at the extreme end of the canyon, was finally reached on February 15, 1911 and the station was opened as of that date.

In the meantime, at the northern end of the line, a branch from Wabuska to Thompson, the smelter of the Mason Valley Mining Company, was constructed during the fall of 1910 and active operations began on the same day the little station of Hudson officially joined the family.

The survey having been completed from Hudson to the shaft of the Nevada-Douglas Copper Mine, the grading contractors pushed their work as rapidly as possible so that the following July surfacing and track laying were under full headway. The road was now completed to the mine and on November 1, 1911 the new station of Ludwig was officially opened.

The Nevada Copper Belt Railroad was at last finished and if we consider Thompson as its most northern point, it ran south through Wabuska to Yerington, Mason and Hudson. Near Hudson the line began to bear west and finally taking a northwesterly course toward the mountains reached Ludwig, the terminus and the headquarters of the Nevada-Douglas Consolidated Copper Company. The completed line resembled the letter "J" with Thompson at the top and Ludwig at the "tail" end. Total distance 40 miles.

At the beginning the railroad was a highly successful operation boasting three steam locomotives and considerable miscellaneous rolling stock which was used to handle local business. When conditions continued to improve there was soon a pressing need for additional motive power and equipment was purchased accordingly.

For passenger and express service the road bought two Hall-Scott motor cars, numbered 21 and 22. The former was built to N.C.B. specifications. In fact Vernon Peterson, veteran of the N.C.B. motor car service, recalls that he was with Mr. John Hickey, who was mechanical engineer for the Copper Belt RR, and Mr. Hall of Hall-Scott, when they laid out the original Hall-Scott motor car design on a table cloth at the U. S. Grant Hotel in San Diego when they were in Southern California inspecting gasoline propelled railway cars.

When the No. 21 was completed at the Hall-Scott shops in Berkeley, Peterson was sent down to take delivery. It was winter in 1911 with seventeen feet of snow in the Sierra Nevada Mountains when Peterson began his return trip with the new Hall-Scott motor car running on its own power over the Southern Pacific tracks. Most of the time the car operated unaided, although occasionally on the steeper grades the S. P. recommended a helper engine, but that was mostly as a safety measure.

Two years later when the #22 was acquired, Peterson went through the same procedure only this time he went back to Utah as this car had been originally built to run on the Salt Lake & Utah, another Orem Line. After serving there about two years it was decided to transfer the #22 to the Nevada Copper Belt and Peterson was selected to make the trip. It was again wintertime and when Peterson and his crew would lay over the car was stored in an S. P. engine house. The #22 it seems, was slightly wider than most S. P. equipment and was quite handy at pulling off the shed doors causing much amusement or consternation depending upon which side you were on.

Somewhere along in the history of the N.C.B. the road acquired a Fairbanks Morse motor car, #20, which was started with a charge of gunpowder, but it was destroyed by fire (probably the roundhouse fire that destroyed other equipment in 1916) and little is known of it.

The schedule, in these early days, consisted of three passenger and nine freight trains per day or a total of twelve round trips every day in the week with the exception of Sunday.

The main stops along the N.C.B. were Wabuska, Yerington, Mason, Hudson and Ludwig. Yerington was formerly known by the colorful handle of "Pizen Switch," but its ambitious citizens dignified the name, at the same time honoring Mr. H. M. Yerington, the colorful superintendent of the historic Virginia & Truckee Railroad. Next a bid was made for the county seat, which at that time was about to move from Dayton. The campaign was successful, too, although Mason, their arch enemy and civic rival, came in just three votes behind.

Hudson, also, had its day when it provided a loading point for the agricultural products that thrived in the rich Smith Valley. Then there was the time of renewed mining activity in the Aurora and Bodie area. Hudson became the rail head and supply center for the workings to the south. Mule skinners and early day truck drivers hauled from Hudson to and from the mines and the resulting activity added revenue to the Nevada Copper Belt Railroad.

Ludwig, which was the headquarters of the large scale operations of the Nevada-Douglas Company was also the site of the Standard Gypsum Plaster Company's plant and these two mining operations made frequent train service both necessary and profitable. The gypsum operation alone provided sizeable loads for the railroad. The gypsum deposit at Ludwig was said to be 4,000 feet in length with a maximum thickness of 200 feet. It was reputed to have been one of the finest deposits of hydrous calcium sulphate in the United States and it offered a possible tonnage of more than 5,000,000 tons.

The Nevada-Douglas as well as the Blue Stone mines reduced the ore right on their property and because of this only the concentrates made the trip to the smelter at Thompson. The settlement of Thompson, where the employes and officials of the company resided became a thriving and somewhat cosmopolitan community. The smelter itself was situated on an eminent height near a natural gateway in the hills. This afforded a draught for the fumes from the high stack.

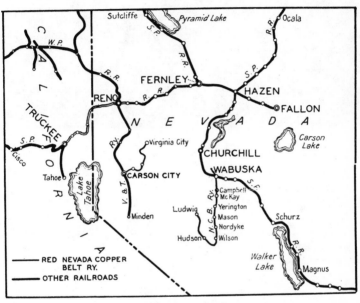

LOCATION MAP

Above: Near Yerington.

Engine house at Mason, Nevada June 1938. Note stub switch in foreground.

No. 5 and train on the Hudson wye.

N.C.B. ore car on an isolated desert siding.

Photo by Jack R. Wagner

All that remains today of the Bluestone Mill are the concrete foundations and a huge pile of tailings.

Nothing remains of the once busy Thompson Smelter.

Gypsum mine at Ludwig as it looked when operating.

and therefore did not interfere with living conditions in the town or the crops on the nearby farms. The plant consisted of two blast furnaces and had a daily capacity of 1700 tons. Typical output figures are these taken from the first eleven months of 1913:

> "210,000 tons of ore reduced to metal; 11,655 ounces being silver, 9069 ounces of gold, and the remainder . . . 13,217,545 pounds of copper."

This data came from the official records of the company up to November 30, 1913.

A direct connection was made with the Southern Pacific at Wabuska, only 2½ miles from Thompson, which facilitated the shipment of outbound copper slabs.

Mr. Ted Bergerson, who later became the district freight and passenger agent in Reno for the Southern Pacific Company, recalled the days when he was the S.P. station agent at Wabuska where the transfer was made. The mines and smelter were running full blast then and the N.C.B. freight interchange to the Southern Pacific amounted to more than one million dollars per month!

Coke from Utah, for the furnaces, at the rate of 18 to 20 cars a day, other fuels, lumber and outgoing copper matte from the smelter all added up to big business. Wabuska, in those days, showed up on the S.P.'s books ten times more profitable than Reno.

Yes, the Nevada Copper Belt was a very busy railroad for in addition to the mining activity there was tributary to the line some 300,000 acres of rich agricultural land located in the Mason, Smith and Antelope Valleys. Most of this land was under irrigation but previous to the advent of the railroad there had been only a limited market for the crops. The coming of the N.C.B. had now connected these farms with the entire railroad system of the United States and if the grower could find a better market for his produce in Chicago or New York he had but to load a car and send it on its way. Soon there developed a vast agricultural business and thereafter it was just as common to see cars of potatoes, onions, hay and livestock as it was copper.

In the salad days of the Nevada Copper Belt Railroad 45 or 50 cars were considered a fair sized train and once (remembered in a photograph that hung in manager Fred Cox' office in Mason) 65 loads went out behind number 5.

In the beginning the Orem brothers, W. C. and Archie J. Orem, were the top officials of the road. The Orems had their headquarters in Salt Lake City and were prominent in western mining circles. Mr. D. MacVichie was appointed general manager of the railroad and C. M. Fraser, superintendent. In August of 1913 Mr. Fraser passed away and F. J. Sullivan, who was at that time auditor, was advanced to the position of superintendent.

A great deal of credit is due Mr. Sullivan for developing business relations with the ranchers throughout the territory served by the railroad. He was always active in obtaining new revenue and his results were phenomenal. Not only was he active in promoting the railroad, but he did much for the advancement of Lyon County. As evidence, in an old brochure titled "Lyon County, Where It Is and What It Contains" we find printed on the inside cover: "For further information write F. J. Sullivan, Mason, Nevada". Mr. Sullivan's abilities, however, did not go unobserved and in November 1914 he was transferred to the Salt Lake & Utah Railroad and the N.C.B.'s loss was their gain.

Mr. P. H. Cook was made the new superintendent and he remained in this position until his retirement in 1937.

As we approach the later life of the Nevada Copper Belt Railroad strange things are beginning to happen. First on April 2, 1925 we find the railroad entering receivership with

J. I. Wilson appointed as receiver. This seems to be an odd procedure as the railroad was operating to capacity and handling some of its heaviest tonnage at the time. It was alleged that various financial manipulations had forced this turn of events. However, receivership or not, traffic continued to be heavy for the next four years. But, then came the beginning of the end. On March 31, 1929 the Thompson smelter closed down. The smelter and the mines were the industries which in the past could always be depended upon for not only the heavy freight revenue of the railroad, but for the general prosperity of the community as well. Now both the tonnage and the payroll were gone.

Conditions didn't improve either and finally when on July 30, 1932 the Standard Gypsum Plant ceased operation the little railroad no longer had reason to visit the fading community of Ludwig. Service was soon discontinued over the nine miles from Hudson to Ludwig and the rails were left to rust and the ties to rot.

With the closing of the mines the railroad began to look toward its agricultural business, but, here, also, was disappointment. Highway trucking had increased and the Copper Belt began to feel the double pinch of poor business conditions and truck competition.

It was in August of 1937 when P. H. Cook retired as superintendent and T. H. Lever filled the vacancy. His term was short, however, as he passed away three years later and was succeeded by L. G. Ellis.

The Canadian born Mr. Ellis began his railroad career on the old Dominion Atlantic Railroad in Nova Scotia in 1900 and since that time had worked on the Colorado Southern and the Southern Pacific. He had come to the Copper Belt in 1914 as chief clerk and chief dispatcher and in 1936 he had been advanced to assistant superintendent. traffic manager and purchasing agent. His superintendency began July 20, 1940.

It was through the efforts and cooperation of Mr. Ellis that many of the facts concerning the Copper Belt have been captured. A precise and exacting man, Ellis took the trouble to record the daily highlights in his journal and the entries in his book provide an accurate and interesting account of life on the Copper Belt.

The boom days were over and the years ahead were to be both trying and discouraging. Superintendent Ellis, together with Mr. H. H. Koehler (pronounced Kay-ler), the auditor, proceeded to hold the little road together and operate on a very slim margin. The railroad which once had sixty persons on its monthly payroll was now down to sixteen. Expenses were cut at every corner, and through the cooperation and loyalty of all remaining employes the Copper Belt carried on.

Mr. J. I. Wilson, the receiver, retired June 30, 1941 and S. C. Bigelow (of the Virginia & Truckee RR) was appointed trustee. It was Bigelow, acting in the capacity of trustee, who brought about the sale of the railroad, and on August 12, 1941 the line was placed on auction to be sold to the highest bidder.

The successful bidder was Mr. Fred D. Parr, San Francisco industrialist and head of the Parr-Richmond Terminal Company.

When the plight of the Nevada Copper Belt Railroad had come to the attention of Mr. Parr he became interested in revitalizing the failing railroad if at all possible. Parr had already earned an impressively successful reputation in the business and shipping world through his establishment of the Parr-McCormack Steamship Line and the Parr Terminal Company. A complete list of his activities would be too lengthy to mention, but if the N.C.B. could be saved here was the man to do it. And so, with the experience, energy and resources of Mr. Fred D. Parr and his organization behind the railroad once again things were looking up.

The policy of the new owners was to continue the operation of the railroad and to develop new business. The sale was, of course, subject to the usual legal formalities, but on February 9, 1942 the Interstate Commerce Commission approved the sale and granted the new company permission to own and operate the road. The trustee was discharged on April 20th and the Parr people began active management and operation of the Nevada Copper Belt Railway Company, as the new company was called.

The new officers consisted of Mr. Fred D. Parr, president; T. A. Goldrick, vice-president and traffic manager; Fred Parr Cox, secretary and general manager; John Parr Cox, controller and purchasing agent; William C. Moorhead, treasurer; H. H. Koehler, auditor, with L. C. Ellis remaining as superintendent.

The new company, under Mr. Parr's direction, attempted to run the little railroad on a business-like basis and made an honest attempt to promote local business. One of the first things they did was to cut off the deadwood at each end of the line. Ever since the gypsum mine at Ludwig had closed down in 1932 the last 9 miles of the road had not been regularly used. The same was true of the two and a half mile extension from Wabuska to what once had been the smelter community of Thompson. These two segments were abandoned and torn up in accordance with permission granted by the I.C.C. on June 23, 1942.

With the unproductive branches cut away the management set out to make the remaining 28 miles a paying proposition. In order to stimulate business the new owners took an active interest in and encouraged local industry even to the point of investing additional capital. It was in line with this policy that the Copper Belt Gypsum Mining Company was formed. Operated by the railroad, this quarry near Yerington, shipped some 100 cars a month over the N.C.B., but when mining expenses increased this activity was discontinued.

In 1942 the railroad people built the Yerington Packing Plant which at that time was the only plant of its kind in the eleven western states packing Federally inspected horse meat for human consumption. For this purpose a number of wild horse camps were operated by the Indians. Horses were captured and driven to the plant for killing and dressing and during the period this plant was operated by the Copper Belt some thirty head a day were used. The meat was packed in iced refrigerator cars and shipped to the San Francisco Bay Area for wartime consumption. This project was sold when even the railroad had to admit that trucks could handle the product just as easily and with less cost to the packer.

In still another attempt to provide revenue for the railroad, the backers were instrumental in establishing a new local industry known as the Fluftrock Company. Railroad officials aided in finding a location and even bought an interest in this plant which for a time turned out building products from silica rock (perlite). This material was used as a light weight aggregate for wall board, plaster and cement. Under heat treatment it would pop like popcorn and fuse itself into a light weight building block. It may have been a good idea, but the plant eventually closed its doors and the machinery was sold. Ironically enough some of the last cars to travel over the N.C.B. hauled away the steam equipment from the factory that might have been the road's best customer.

The days of heavy tonnage by rail were now over and about the only products to still move by train were cattle, potatoes, hay and onions from the local ranches. But, all of that traffic didn't fall to the railroad as many farmers preferred to haul by truck and soon the management found it necessary to remove some of the trains. In line with this application was made to the Nevada Public Service Commission in 1944 for a franchise to operate a truck from Yerington to Wabuska to haul mail, express and less-than-carload lot freight. Permission was granted and from then on the locomotives were steamed up only when there were cars to move. Since this was all too seldom, the road, in an effort to further curtail expenses, purchased a 30 ton Plymouth gasoline locomotive. For what rail traffic remained with the Copper Belt this little engine was more than adequate, in fact for one period the steam locomotives were out of service for almost three months.

The passenger department supplied another nonproductive service and in 1945 it became necessary to eliminate passenger schedules entirely.

The Nevada Copper Belt Railway Company was going deeper and deeper in the red and there was no indication that conditions would ever get better. There was nothing more to do but suspend service entirely and so on August 21, 1946 the N.C.B. formally applied to the Nevada Public Service Commission for authority to abandon its entire line. When the hearing was held in Carson City protests were filed by the Lyon County Farm Bureau and the Smith Valley Rotary Club. In their objections the protestors contended:

> ". . . that the production of hay, grain, potatoes and other farm produce has increased yearly, and the acreage of land under cultivation can be increased if proper use of water is made for irrigation purposes. To deprive the ranchers of railroad shipping facilities would seriously handicap the whole agricultural area in marketing its crops in competition with other areas. Freight rates would

probably be higher; perishable products would not be shipped during the winter months on account of danger of frost if transported by trucks."

No doubt the objections were valid ones, but these same farmers had not seen fit to ship by rail in the past and there was no guarantee that they would do so in the future.

Another protesting witness talked about the loss it would be to the mining industry if the road was allowed to go out of business. He predicted that increased amounts of ore would be shipped from the mines near Mason and that the future operation of those properties was dependent upon the railroad. Perhaps true, but let's get back to reality. At the time of the hearing there was a large copper company engaged in development work near Yerington, but they either would not or could not offer any information as to whether or not another mining boom could be expected on the Copper Belt. Sure, mining talk was plentiful around Mason and Yerington just as it is around any town that has been touched by the prosperity of a big bonanza. The barber shop and pool room commentators could tell you that such and such a big company has a representative in town picking up options. "Yes, sir, it won't be long now," they'd say. But, let's look at the record. During the first seven months of 1946 only one carload of ore was loaded at Yerington and none of the mines were being worked at the time of the hearing.

Then there was the matter of the roadbed. While much of it was still in fair condition there were nevertheless many ties that needed replacing if safe operation was to be assured. That figure alone amounted to $72,000 . . . and when you consider that the entire population served by the line was less than 1600 at the time it just wasn't worth it.

No, there wasn't much to look forward to. Sure, the

mines *might* come back and the farmers *might* see the error of their ways and decide to ship by rail . . . and then again they *might* not. Any good business man would consider it justifiable to give the whole thing up as a bad job. The Nevada Public Service Commission saw it that way, too, and in their decision handed down December 30, 1946, they stated:

> "It is the opinion of this Commission that the proposed abandonment will not subject the communities to serious injury and that the continued operation would impose an undue burden upon the applicant . . ."

An application was also filed with the Interstate Commerce Commission in Washington, D. C. and their findings were substantially the same. The official date of suspension was set for March 24, 1947.

There were, however, a few people seriously concerned with the loss of the railroad. Among these were Franklin H. Koehler, an attorney-at-law and James E. O'Connor, a public accountant. In Yerington these men shared the same office as well as the same feelings. Maybe they were railfans at heart . . . or maybe they could see possibilities in the N.C.B. that others couldn't . . . at any rate they had hopes of continuing the operation of the railroad. They were willing to put all of their resources behind the project and sought additional support from the community. The local investors, however, couldn't quite see the same possibilities so the deal never jelled. Koehler and O'Connor have since chalked it up as just another lost cause, but they still admit that they would have considered it a dividend paid if they could have just blown the whistle.

Perhaps by now some of the other townspeople feel the same way because no longer does the throaty voice of number 5 reach out across the clear desert air and no longer do the round, mellow tones of her bell announce her arrival from Wabuska. Yerington never sees a locomotive these days and to a new generation a train is a wonder from the outside world seen only on infrequent vacations or in picture books. The N.C.B. has joined the ghosts of the miners who once toiled in the underground rooms of the Nevada-Douglas and the glory holes of the Blue Stone.

All is desert and motortrucks. The N.C.B. is dead.

THE NEVADA COPPER BELT RAILWAY COMPANY

Incorporated March 22, 1909
Abandoned March 24, 1947

TECRASILK PHOTOS

Cattle on the track!

Nevada Copper Belt Waycar-caboose No. 3. Color: red.

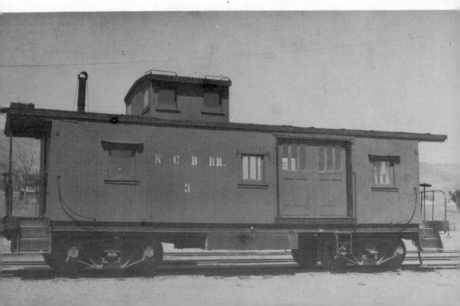

N.C.B. connected with the Southern Pacific at Wabuska, Nev.

No. 5 at the Junction. Left to right: Jack Devine, engineer; J. H. Thompson, conductor; Earl Person, S.P. agent at Wabuska; G. M. Ludwick, brakeman, and Vernon Peterson, fireman.

Photos by Jack R. Wagner

Once the road went on to Ludwig, but in 1947 when this photo was taken Hudson was the end of the line.

The entire population of Hudson, Nevada, January, 1947.

Photo by Jack R. Wagner

No. 2 was a Lima 2-8-0 built in 1911. Photo taken at Mason, Nevada, February 1, 1947.

Baldwin Locomotive Works

The N.C.B. No. 3 was sold to the Sierra Railroad where it became their No. 24.

Her days were numbered when this photo of the 5 spot was taken February 1, 1947.

During periods of slack business all trains were handled by this 30 ton Plymouth gasoline locomotive. (1947)

Photo by Jack Wagner

An N.C.B. eastbound freight in the Walker River Canyon

Making up a train at Hudson.

Above: Round house at Mason, Nevada.

Right: Engineer Jack Devine.

Photos by Jack R. Wagner

Combination motor cars Numbers 21 and 22.

Loading mail and express at Yerington.

Passenger service on the NCB was provided by Hall-Scott motor cars No. 21 and No. 22. The No. 21 was purchased from the railroad by Bay Area railfans Richard Reynolds, Eldon Lucy and Arthur Lloyd. It was completely reconditioned in 1965 and can be seen at the California Railway Museum at Rio Vista Junction. It still contains, in working order, the original engine which was the third engine built by Hall-Scott.

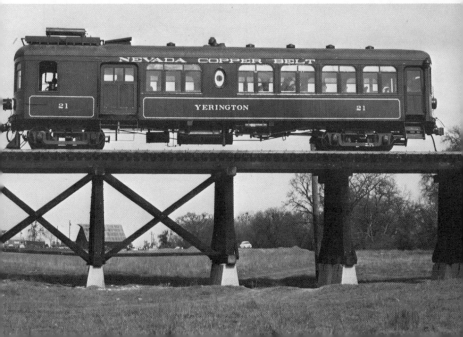

NEVADA COPPER BELT RAILROAD COMPANY
TRIP PASS

No. 2356

PASS_____

_____ ADDRESS _____

ACCOUNT_____

FROM _____ TO _____ & RETURN

VALID WHEN COUNTERSIGNED BY
P. H. COOK OR L. G. ELLIS

REQUESTED BY

James F Berryhull
PRESIDENT

DATE ISSUED_____192___ EXPIRES _____192___

Pass and tickets used on
the Nevada Copper Belt
Railroad.

NEVADA COPPER BELT R. R. Co.
MASON
—TO—
LUDWIG

3841

Not good unless dated on back with station stamp.
Good only for contin-
uous passage on or one
day after sale date.
Liability for baggage
limited to $100
Form T-7

Traffic Manager

NEVADA COPPER BELT R. R. CO.
AGENT'S STUB.
First Class One Way Ticket.
NOT GOOD FOR PASSAGE.

Date Issued_____

From_____

To_____

Price_____

Form T 1	HALF FARE
8253	IF PUNCHED HERE.

NEVADA COPPER BELT RAILROAD COMPANY
FIRST CLASS ONE WAY TICKET
GOOD FOR ONE CONTINUOUS PASSAGE

From_____

To_____

Good One Day from date stamped on back.

Form T 1	HALF FARE	
8253	IF PUNCHED HERE.	*Traffic Manager*

The yards at Hudson.

A lonely outpost on the N.C.B.

Station and freight shed, Yerington, Nevada.

Photos by Jack R. Wagner

"Bank corner" in once busy Mason, Nevada.

This stubby car was once used as a smoking car behind motor car No. 20. Its dimensions were only 7½ feet wide and 18 feet long.

Photos by Jack R. Wagner

Wild horses were once captured by the Indians and driven to a packing plant operated by the Nevada Copper Belt Railroad.

Below: Cattle loading facilities on the N.C.B.

Photos by Jack R. Wagner

A Virginia & Truckee crew talks with the N.C.B. prior to their taking over the No. 5.

Below: Near the end. N.C.B. manager, Fred Cox, M. T. Lummus of the A. D. Schader Company (Railroad Contractors) and Nick Perris, section foreman, discuss plans for tearing up the rails. Perris had been with the N.C.B. since it was first built. It was Perris who laid the first tie.

Photos by Jack R. Wagner

NEVADA COPPER BELT RAILROAD COMPANY

TIME TABLE No. 26

To take effect Sunday, June 2, 1918, at 12:01 a. m., Pacific Time

For the government and information of employes only, and not intended for the use of the public. The Company reserves the right to vary from this schedule as circumstances may require.

W. C. OREM,
PRESIDENT

ARCHIE J. OREM,
GENERAL SUPERINTENDENT

P. H. COOK,
SUPERINTENDENT

NEVADA COPPER BELT RAILROAD COMPANY

EASTWARD   TIME TABLE   WESTWARD

No. 26 — JUNE 2, 1918

WATER WYE FUEL SCALES	8 Passenger (1st Class) Leave Daily	6 Passenger Leave Daily Except Sunday	4 Passenger Leave Daily	2 Passenger Leave Daily	Distance from Wabuska	STATIONS	Distance from Ludwig	1 Passenger (1st Class) Arrive Daily	3 Passenger Arrive Daily	5 Passenger Arrive Daily Except Sunday	7 Passenger Arrive Daily	CAR CAPACITY SIDINGS
WYS 0	1:00 P.M.		4:00 P.M.	9:15 P.M.	0.0	D WABUSKA	37.8	8:50 P.M.	3:30 P.M.		12:30 P.M.	50
						6.7						
	f 1:15		f 4:15	f 9:30	6.7	McKAY	31.1	f 8:25	f 3:07		f 12:07 P.M.	6
						4.8						
	s 1:30		s 4:30	s 9:45	11.5	D YERINGTON	26.3	s 8:12	s 2:57		f 11:57	10
						2.6						
WYO	1:40 P.M.	8:00 A.M.	4:40 P.M.	9:55 P.M.	14.1	D MASON	23.7	8:05 P.M.	2:50 P.M.	11:05 A.M.	11:50 A.M.	50
						4.2						
		f 8:07			18.3	NORDYKE	19.5			f 10:55		8
						3.7						
		f 8:13			22.0	WILSON	15.8			f 10:48		8
						6.8						
WY		s 8:37			28.8	D HUDSON	9.0			s 10:27		10
						3.4						
		f 8:47			32.2	COLONY	5.6			f 10:12		10
						4.4						
Y					36.6	WYE	1.2					
						1.2						
W		9:15 A.M.			37.8	D LUDWIG	0.0			10:00 A.M.		
						37.8						
	Arrive Daily	Arrive Daily Except Sunday	Arrive Daily	Arrive Daily				Leave Daily	Leave Daily	Leave Daily Except Sunday	Leave Daily	40
	21	18	21	21		AVERAGE SPEED PER HOUR		18	21	22	21	
	(.40)	(1.15)	(.40)	(.40)		TIME OVER DISTRICT		(.45)	(.40)	(1.05)	(.40)	

WESTWARD TRAINS ARE SUPERIOR TO TRAINS OF THE SAME CLASS IN THE OPPOSITE DIRECTION.
No. 5 WILL WAIT AT LUDWIG UNTIL No. 6 ARRIVES. ALL TRAINS WILL STOP AT WARREN AND CAMPBELL CROSSING ON FLAG.

OLDEST TIMETABLE IN EFFECT

"The question has come up before concerning 'What line has the oldest timetable still in effect?' Nevada Copper Belt Railroad seems to claim this distinction. Its last employees' card, No. 26, appeared June 2, 1918. To date forty supplements have been issued to supersede it, but the same schedule has not been superseded by timetable No. 27."

From the Railroad Journal, August 1942

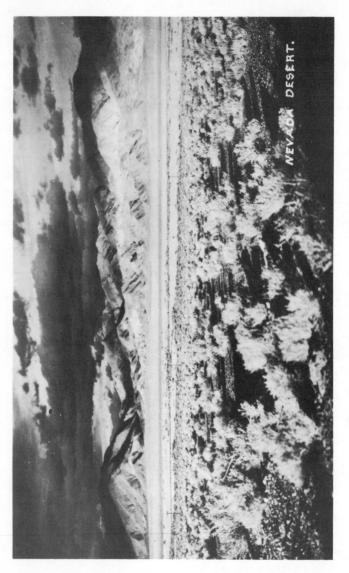

NEVADA DESERT.

All is desert and motor trucks . . . the N.C.B. is dead.

APPENDIX

Short line locomotives, like the men who run them, are individualists with strong personalities of their own; some are the "roving kind" working for a time on one railroad, then appearing on the rails of another short line many miles away. Naturally exact information on such a mobile subject is hard to obtain—even company records are not always complete.

Tracing the ancestry and career of the iron horse has become the hobby of many railroad historians and serious collectors of railroad material, and by comparing the various lists over a period of time and weeding out the discrepancies, a fairly accurate history has been obtained.

It is in this spirit that we present the locomotive rosters of the seven short line railroads we have dealt with in this book. We gratefully acknowledge the help and effort that has gone before and while time will, no doubt, prove certain inaccuracies subject to correction, the following list is presented as the most complete roster available at this time.

THE AUTHOR.

Locomotives of the California Western Railroad

REVISED ROSTER

Number	Type	Builder	Serial	Date	Driv.	Cyl.	Tract. Force	Boil. Pres.	Tot. Wt.
1	2-4-2T	Baldwin	# 7831	1886	42	12x20	7560	130	56000
			Sold 1906 to Standish & Hickey, became Calif. Lumber Co. No. 2.						
2	2-4-4T	Baldwin	# 8852	1887	42	12x20	7560	130	62000
			Sold 1910 to Irvine Muir Lumber Co., No. 2. Became a 2-4-2T when trailing truck switched with No. 3. Fort Bragg Lumber Co. No. 2.						
2	0-4-2T	Baldwin	#18618	1901	50	17x24	18800	160	92700
			Ex-California State Belt Line No. 2, purchased prior to 1912. Scrapped 1920.						
3	2-2-2T	Baldwin	. . .	1884	42	14x18	. . .	. . .	70000
			Sold 1918 to Mendocino Lumber Co. No. 2. Became a 2-4-4T when trailing truck switched with No. 2.						
4	4-4-0	Hinkley	. . .	1883	57	16x24	. . .	. . .	115000*
			*Weight of engine and tender. Scrapped 1914.						
5	4-6-0	Schen.	# 1301	1880	57	18x24	20200	165	90000
			Purchased 1906, scrapped 1923. Ex-SP of Ariz. 22, SP 102, 1605, 2042.						
6	0-4-0	Mason	# 245	1867	48	14x22	7636	100	52000
			Purchased 1906, scrapped 1915. Ex-California Pacific 1, SP 1114, 1002.						
7	2-6-2T	Baldwin	#33390	1909	44	15x22	15780	165	102000
			Renumbered 17 in 1924.						
8	4-6-0	McKay & Aldus	. . .	1867	57	18x24	20200	165	102000
			Purchased 1910, renumbered 38 in 1924. Ex-Central Pacific 39, SP 1529, 2002.						

No.	Type	Builder	Builder No.	Year		Cylinders			
9	3T Shay	Lima	# 2547	1912	32	11x12	25800	200	120000

Sold 1914 to White River Lumber Co. No. 9. Enumclaw, Wash.

| 11 | 2-6-2T | Baldwin | #39551 | 1913 | 44 | 15x22 | 16300 | 170 | 110000 |

Scrapped 1947.

| 12 | 2-6-2T | Baldwin | #41922 | 1915 | 44 | 15x22 | 16300 | 170 | 110000 |

Scrapped 1950.

| 14 | 2-6-2T | Baldwin | #58050 | 1924 | 44 | 15x24 | 18750 | 180 | 111380 |

Ex-California Fruit Exchange No. 1, Graegle, Calif. Purchased 1938, sold to Bert Rudolph, Willits, 1956.

| 17 | 2-6-2T | Baldwin | #33390 | 1909 | 44 | 15x22 | 15780 | 165 | 102000 |

Ex-No. 7, scrapped 1938.

| 21 | 2-6-2 | Baldwin | #53277 | 1920 | 44 | 18x24 | 30000 | 200 | 140000 |

Sold 1950 to Pan American Engineering.

| 22 | 2-6-2 | Baldwin | #54898 | 1921 | 44 | 18x24 | 30000 | 200 | 139000 |

Scrapped 1952.

| 23 | 2-6-2 | Baldwin | #57553 | 1923 | 44 | 18x24 | 30000 | 200 | 141000 |

Scrapped 1950.

| 36 | 4-6-0 | Baldwin | # 9298 | 1888 | 52 | 19x24 | 22600 | 160 | 110000 |

Purchased 1918 from Colorado Midland No. 36. Sold 1929 to Little River Redwood Co., No. 7.

| 38 | 4-6-0 | McKay & Aldus | . . . | 1867 | 57 | 18x24 | 20200 | 165 | 102000 |

Ex-No. 8. Scrapped 1942.

| 41 | 0-6-0 | Baldwin | #18760 | 1901 | 50 | 16x24 | 14960 | 160 | 72000 |

Purchased 1922, scrapped 1937. Ex-Arizona & New Mexico No. 16, Ex-El Paso & Southwestern No. 30.

LOCOMOTIVES OF THE CALIFORNIA WESTERN RAILROAD (CONTINUED)

Number	Type	Builder	Serial	Date	Driv.	Cyl.	Tract. Force	Boil.Pres.	Tot. Wt.
41	2-8-0	Baldwin	#53205	1920	42	18x22	26010	180	121000

Purchased 1944, scrapped 1952. Ex-Lamm Lumber Co. No. 3, Modoc Point, Oregon.

Number	Type	Builder	Serial	Date	Driv.	Cyl.	Tract. Force	Boil.Pres.	Tot. Wt.
44	2-8-2	Baldwin	#61306	1930	44	19x24	31900	190	158700

Purchased 1944, scrapped 1952. Ex-Lamm Lumber Co. No. 3, Modoc Point, Oregon.

MOTOR CARS (Skunks)

Number	Type	Builder	Serial	Date	Driv.	Cyl.	Tract. Force	Boil.Pres.	Tot. Wt.
M-80	Gasoline	Mack Motor Car Co.		1925	...	...	30 passengers		20000

Wrecked 1959, rebuilt 1961, wrecked 1964 and retired.

Number	Type	Builder	Serial	Date	Driv.	Cyl.	Tract. Force	Boil.Pres.	Tot. Wt.
M-100	Diesel	Edwards Motor Car Co.		1926	...	...	36 passengers		38000

Purchased 1934, rebuilt 1956. Ex-Morehead & North Fork RR, Morehead, Kentucky. Wrecked in 1964, rebuilt in 1965 adding 6 feet more in length.

Number	Type	Builder	Serial	Date	Driv.	Cyl.	Tract. Force	Boil.Pres.	Tot. Wt.
M-200	Gasoline	Skagit Steel Co.		1926	...	...	55 passengers		46000

Purchased 1941. Ex-Trona Railway No. 22, Trona, Calif.

Number	Type	Builder	Serial	Date	Driv.	Cyl.	Tract. Force	Boil.Pres.	Tot. Wt.
M-300	Diesel	American Car & Foundry		1935	...	...	83 passengers		52600

64" long. Ex-Aberdeen & Rockfish, ex-Salt Lake, Garfield & Western M-3, purchased 1963, rebuilt in 1964 to eliminate baggage section.

MISC. EQUIPMENT: (disposition unknown)

42 (Passenger) Combination, wooden frame, built about 1891. Purchased in 1908 from N. B. Livermore. A former San Pedro, Los Angeles & Salt Lake RR car.

43 (Observation-passenger) Same as above.

44 (Coach) Wooden frame. Former Central Pacific car #1185, purchased from SP in 1914. Misc. 11, freight cars 12.

Locomotives of the California Western Railroad (Continued)

Fort Bragg to Willits, Calif. — 40.0 miles (main line)

Number of employees varies from a low of 47 in the winter to a high of 66 during the summer months.

The California Western is a subsidiary of the Boise Cascade Corporation. Boise Cascade acquired the line through purchase of the Union Lumber Company in January, 1969.

Most noticeable change since the previous edition of SHORT LINE JUNCTION has been the establishment of regularly scheduled steam powered passenger service and the acquisition of additional equipment to provide this service (see Roster changes). Inaugural trip was made on July 9, 1965 and was an immediate success as a tourist attraction. Steam trains run during spring and summer. For reserved tickets, timetables and charter information write California Western Railroad, Box 907-B, Fort Bragg, California 95437.

Roster changes and comments:

Steam

Number	Type	Builder	Serial	Date	Driv.	Cyl.	Tract. Force	Boil.Pres.	Tot. Wt.
45	2-8-2	Baldwin	#58045	1926	44	19x24	20000	180	120000
	Mikado, formerly Owens-Oregon Lumber Co. No. 3; Medford Corp. No. 3, purchased by Cal. Western 1965.								
46	2-6-6-2	Baldwin	#62064	1937	44	18x24x24	42500	200	247000
	Mallet, purchased from Rayonier, Inc. at Hoquiam, Washington 1969.								

LOCOMOTIVES OF THE CALIFORNIA WESTERN RAILROAD (CONTINUED)

Number	Type	Builder	Serial	Date	Driv.	Cyl.	Tract. Force	Boil. Pres.	Tot. Wt.
			DIESEL ELECTRIC						
51*	B-B	Baldwin	#74408	1949	40	750 hp	50000	...	200000
52*	B-B	Baldwin	#74409	1949	40	750 hp	50000	...	200000
53	B-B	Baldwin	#74193	1949	40	1000 hp	58750	...	235000

Ex-U.S. Government W8380, purchased 1956 through Pan American Engineering Co.

54*	B-B	Baldwin	#75823	1953	40	1200 hp	72000	...	240000

Formerly Wabash #307, purchased from Crown Crankshaft Co.

* Wrecked in January, 1970 and scrapped on the spot.

55	RS-12	Baldwin	#76024			(Equipped with heavy duty Westinghouse
56	RS-12	Baldwin	#76105			(370 traction motors

Both of the above units were originally built for the McCloud River RR (#32 and #33). Cal. Western operated them on lease for a time to fill out the power roster after the January, 1970 wreck. They were purchased from their owner, the Chrome Crankshaft Co., in Oct. 1970.

COACHES

Along with steam locomotives #45 and #46 additional coaches have been acquired to provide increased passenger capacity. These cars were acquired from the Erie-Lackawanna Railroad, #2300, #2332, #2343 and #2345. Built in 1926 from designs by L. B. Stillwell of about 1912. Each coach is 72 feet long.

Railroad also has on hand 1 former SP commute coach of the Harrimon 2200 series built in 1917. Acquired 1968.

FORT BRAGG RAILROAD

Predecessor to the California Western. Built north of Fort Bragg along Pudding Creek to Glen Blair in 1886.

No.	Type	Cylinders	Drivers	Weight	T.F.	B.P.	Builder	Date, No.
1	2-4-2T	12x20	42	56,000	7,560	130	BLW	1886–7831
	Named "Sequoia," became CW with same number.							
2	2-4-4T	12x20	42	62,000	7,560	130	BLW	1887–8852
	Became CW with same number.							
3	2-4-2T	14x18	42	70,000			BLW	1884
	Purchased second hand, 1895, became CW with same number.							
4	4-0	16x24	57	115,000*			Hinkley	1883
	Purchased second hand, 1904, became CW with same number.							
	*Weight of engine and tender.							

UNION LUMBER COMPANY

(locomotives operated independently by the Union Lumber Co.)

No.	Type	Cylinders	Drivers	Weight	T.F.	B.P.	Builder	Date, No.
1	0-4-0T							
	Ex-Glen Blair Redwood Co. This engine acquired for display purposes 1949. Now at Union Lumber Co. logging museum.							
2	2T Shay	10x12	29	65,900	16,000	180	Lima	1906–1838
	Ex-Glen Blair Redwood Co. No. 2, scrapped 1950.							

SHIPS OWNED BY THE NATIONAL STEAMSHIP COMPANY

Shipping subsidiary of the Union Lumber Co. Incorporated June 24, 1901.

"National City" 310 tons, built at San Francisco by Alex Hay in 1888. Purchased in 1906 and sold in 1918 to Peru.

"Brunswick" 512 tons, built at North Bend, Oregon, by A. W. Simpson in 1898, bought in 1903 and sold in 1931 to the Hammond Lumber Co.

"Coquille River" 415 tons, built at Prosper, Oregon, by Sudden & Christenson in 1896, bought in 1908 and sold in 1925 to Russell J. Hubbard.

"Arctic" 392 tons, built at Bay City, Oregon, by Charles G. White in 1901, bought in 1908 and wrecked off Point Arena in 1922.

"Noyo" (No. 1) 316 tons, built by Bendix Shipyard, Humboldt Bay in 1888, wrecked off Point Arena in 1914.

"Noyo" (No. 2) 1,419 tons, built at San Francisco by the Union Iron Works in 1913. She was originally the "Aroline," then the "Admiral Goodrich," and renamed the "Noyo." Purchased 1923, wrecked off Point Arena on June 10, 1935.

"Noyo" (No. 3) 1,484 tons, built at Seattle, Wash., in 1920, originally the "Griffdu," renamed the "Noyo" when bought in June, 1935, sold on November 28, 1940, to Thailand.

"Coquell" — No records.

The last two Noyos were steel ships, the others were wooden.

LOCOMOTIVES OF THE YREKA WESTERN
(YREKA RAILROAD)

Number	Type	Builder	Serial	Date	Driv.	Cyl.	Tract. Force	Boil. Pres.	Tot. Wt.
1	2-4-2T	Baldwin	# 9648	1889	46	12x18	6300	130	52000
	Scrapped 1930.								
2	4-4-0	Cooke	# 1725	1886	61	18x24	13540	125	64000
	Ex-Oregon Pacific No. 11, ex-Oregon Central & Eastern No. 11, ex-Corvallis & Eastern No. 11. Purchased 1898, scrapped 1918.								
3	4-6-0	Schen.	# 1639	1882	57	18x24	16230	140	89100
	Ex-SP de M No. 48, SP 207, 1681, 2093. Purchased 1906, scrapped 1932.								
7	0-6-0	Brooks	#54563	1914	51	20x24	28000	175	147000
	ex-State Belt RR No. 7. Purchased 1944, scrapped 1955.								
8	0-6-0	Baldwin	#43670	1916	51	20x24	28000	175	140000
	Ex-State Belt RR No. 8. Purchased 1944, scrapped 1956.								
9	2-6-2	Baldwin	#18596	1901	44	16x24	19000	160	107000
	Ex-McCloud River No. 9. Purchased 1936, sold 1944 to Amador Central, No. 9, Nezperce & Idaho No. 9 (?).								
10	2-6-2	Baldwin	#18674	1901	44	16x24	21330	180	107000
	Ex-McCloud River RR No. 10. Purchased about 1930, scrapped 1944.								
18	2-8-2	Baldwin	#41709	1914	48	20x28	35700	180	178400
	Ex-McCloud River RR No. 18. Purchased 1956. Recently reconditioned new lagging and grate area, flues and ICC inspection good through Sept. 1, 1971.								

LOCOMOTIVES OF THE YREKA WESTERN (CONTINUED)

Number	Type	Builder	Serial	Date	Driv.	Cyl.	Tract. Force	Boil. Pres.	Tot. Wt.
19	2-8-2	Baldwin	#42000	1915	48	20x28	35700	180	178400

Ex-McCloud River RR No. 19. Purchased 1953. Stored serviceable but requires ICC inspection for operation.

Number	Type	Builder	Serial	Date	Driv.	Cyl.	Tract. Force	Boil. Pres.	Tot. Wt.
94	3T Shay	Lima	# 2943	1917	32	12x12	26850	200	129200

Ex-Long Bell Lumber Co. No. 94. Purchased 1943, scrapped 1946.

Number	Type	Builder	Serial	Date	Driv.	Cyl.	Tract. Force	Boil. Pres.	Tot. Wt.
100	2-8-2	Brooks	#61857	1920	48	20x28	36680	185	176000

Ex-Portland, Astoria & Pacific No. 100, ex-Weed Lumber Co. No. 100, ex-Long Bell Lumber Co. No. 100. Purchased 1955, sold and shipped to South San Francisco Scrap Metals Co., Nov. 16, 1955.

SUPPLEMENTARY INFORMATION – 1971

Yreka to Montague, California – 8.5 miles (main line)
Number of employees: 8

At the conclusion of Chapter 2 the fate of the Yreka Western Railroad was in doubt as owner A. D. Schader had died on December 15, 1954. However, the railroad was soon purchased from the Schader estate by Willis B. Kyle and was transferred with court approval on August 6, 1956. Mr. Kyle is listed as the chief stockholder, there being only two others and both are members of his family.

Roster additions:

DIESEL ELECTRIC

No.	Type	Serial	Builder	Driv.	Tractive Effort	Total Weight
602	B-B	#17230 SW-8	EMD	40	62000	100 tons

Bought from the now abandoned Bamburger Railway Co., Salt Lake City, 1955.

No.	Type	Serial	Builder	Driv.	Tractive Effort	Total Weight
604	B-B	RS-6	Alco	40	59000	97 tons

Bought from Portland Traction Co., Portland, Ore., 1965.

MISC. ROLLING STOCK:

Former SP 128, a heavyweight Pullman with observation deck built in 1928. Used on NWP until 1962 as the private business car of former NWP VP and Gen. Mgr. G. L. Morrison. Now used in excursion passenger service on the Yreka Western. Has kitchen, berths, office and six wheeled roller bearing trucks. Still carries the name "Santa Rosa".

ATSF business car built 1936. Formerly used by ATSF Division Superintendent Sid Roger of Fresno. Heavyweight, four wheeled trucks with observation deck and complete facilities. Acquired 1966. Reconditioned by Yreka Western. YW No. 409.

Yreka Western No. 13, formerly Great Northern No. 18. Acquired 1960. Now used as residence car for Yreka Western owner Willis Kyle when in town. Formerly used by G.N. on the Portland-Seattle run.

Two ex-Daylight streamlined lightweight articulated passenger cars from SP.

One caboose.

All above equipment is stored in operating condition at Yreka.

Correction: On page 45 we referred to Vince Delano in error. It should read Vince (or Vincent A.) Gualano.

Locomotives of the McCloud River Railroad

Number	Type	Builder	Serial	Date	Driv.	Cyl.	Tract. Force	Boil. Pres.	Tot. Wt.
1	2-6-0	Baldwin	#11627	1891	50	16x24	14600	140	78000
	Renumbered No. 12. Originally Calif. Ry. No. 2.								
2	Heisler 3T	Sterns	.....	1897(?)	40	18x15	24000	170	140000
3	Heisler			(supposedly same as #2)				...	......
4	2-6-2	Baldwin	#16239	1898	44	16x24	19000	160	96000
	Scrapped 1939.								
5	0-6-0T	Baldwin	#17684	1900	40	11½&19x30	17850	200	75500
	Sold to Lystul-Lawson Logging Co. Retained number. See No. 6.								
6	0-6-0T	Baldwin	#17685	1900	40	11½&19x30	17850	200	75500
	Engines 5 and 6 were built as a single 0-6-6-0T double ender. Operated as No. 6. They were later separated and used as two engines, 5 and 6. No. 6 was later sold to Atkinson Construction Co. Retained number.								
7	4-6-0	...	.....	.....	..	.....	.....	..	......
	Sold to Hetch Hetchy RR (?).								
8	2-6-2	Baldwin	#18595	1901	44	16x24	19000	160	107000
	Sold to Amador Central RR, 1939. Became No. 7								
9	2-6-2	Baldwin	#18596	1901	44	16x24	19000	160	107000
	Same as No. 8. Sold to Yreka RR (#9) Amador Central (#9), Nezperce & Idaho (#9).								

LOCOMOTIVES OF THE McCLOUD RIVER RAILWAY (CONTINUED)

Number	Type	Builder	Serial	Date	Driv.	Cyl.	Tract. Force	Boil. Pres.	Tot. Wt.
10	2-6-2	Baldwin	#18674	1901	44	16x24	21330	180	107000
		Sold to Yreka RR. (#10) Scrapped by Yreka RR.							
11	2-6-2	Baldwin	#23875	1904	44	13&22x24	21240	200	147000
		Sold to Alaska Junk Co., scrapped 1939.							
12	2-6-0	Baldwin	#11627	1891	50	16x24	14600	140	78000
		Formerly No. 1. Scrapped 1932.							
14†	2-8-2	Baldwin	#30850	1907	48	20x28	35700	180	179000
15†	2-8-2	Baldwin	#30851	1907	48	20x28	35700	180	179000
		Same as No. 14.							
16	Shay	Lima	#2401	1911	36	14½x15	40450	200	180000
		Sold to Fruit Growers Supply Co. in 1924. Became No. 4.							
16	2-8-2	Baldwin	#39394	1913	40	40-20½x28	35500	170	176000
		Ex-Silver Falls Timber Co. No. 101.							
17	Shay	Lima	#2402	1911	36	14½x15	40450	200	180000
		Same as first No. 16. Sold to Fruit Growers Supply Co. in 1924. Became No. 5.							
17	2-8-2	Baldwin	#42912	1916	48	20½x28	35400	170	179700
		Ex-Pacific Portland Cement No. 102, purchased 1942.							
18*†	2-8-2	Baldwin	#41709	1914	48	20x28	35700	180	178400

Locomotives of the McCloud River River Railroad (Continued)

Number	Type	Builder	Serial	Date	Driv.	Cyl.	Tract. Force	Boil. Pres.	Tot. Wt.
19	2-8-2	Baldwin	#42000	1915	48	20x28	35700	180	178400

Same as No. 18. Said to have been purchased from a Mexican mining company. Sold to Yreka Western 1953.

Number	Type	Builder	Serial	Date	Driv.	Cyl.	Tract. Force	Boil. Pres.	Tot. Wt.
20 †	2-6-2	Baldwin	#57617	1924	46	17x24	23700	185	132000
21 †	2-6-2	Baldwin	#57618	1924	46	17x24	23700	185	132000

Same as No. 20.

Number	Type	Builder	Serial	Date	Driv.	Cyl.	Tract. Force	Boil. Pres.	Tot. Wt.
22 †	2-6-2	Schen.	#66316	1925	46	17x24	23700	185	127000
23†	2-6-2	Schen.	#66317	1925	46	17x24	23700	185	127000

Same as No. 22.

Number	Type	Builder	Serial	Date	Driv.	Cyl.	Tract. Force	Boil. Pres.	Tot. Wt.
24 †	2-6-2	Schen.	#66434	1925	46	19x24	28800	180	144000
25*†	2-6-2	Schen.	#66435	1925	46	19x24	28800	180	144000

Same as No. 24.

Number	Type	Builder	Serial	Date	Driv.	Cyl.	Tract. Force	Boil. Pres.	Tot. Wt.
26*	2-8-2	Brooks (American)	#55492	1915	48	20x28	...	...	195000

Ex-Copper River & Northwestern No. 72. Purchased 1938.

Number	Type	Builder	Serial	Date	Driv.	Cyl.	Tract. Force	Boil. Pres.	Tot. Wt.
27	2-8-2	Brooks (American)	#57291	1917	48	20x28	...	...	195000

Same as No. 26. Ex-Copper River & Northwestern No. 73. Purchased 1938.

28†	Diesel-elect.	Baldwin	R. S. Type	....	1500 HP	....	150 Tons
29†	Diesel-elect.	Baldwin	R. S. Type	....	1500 HP	....	150 Tons
30†	Diesel-elect.	Baldwin	S. Type	....	1200 HP	....	120 Tons
31†	Diesel-elect.	Baldwin	S. Type	....	800 HP	....	100 Tons
32†	Diesel-elect.	Baldwin	R. S. Type	....	1200 HP	....	120 Tons
33†	Diesel-elect.	Baldwin	R. S. Type	....	1200 HP	....	120 Tons

Note: (A) All Diesels are equipped with multiple-unit controls. Nos. 29, 32 and 33 have Dynamic brakes.

(B) *The railroad now has available for operation three steam locomotives (Nos. 18, 25, 26.). These are leased to the McCloud Lumber Company for use in their logging operations.

(C) †Purchased new.

(D) Steam locomotives Nos. 16, 20, 21 sold to Purdy Co. for scrap Nov. 23, 1955.

Nos. 22, 24 sold to South San Francisco Scrap Metals Company Nov. 16, 1955.

MISCELLANEOUS EQUIPMENT: #100, Ford station wagon with rail tires. #101, Ford station wagon with rail tires. Freight cars, 305. Miscellaneous cars, 20.

SUPPLEMENTARY INFORMATION – 1971

McCloud to Burney, Calif. – 81 miles (main line not totally operated)
Number of employees: 65

The McCloud Lumber Company and controlling interest in the McCloud River Railroad were purchased by U.S. Plywood-Champion Papers, Inc. in 1963. Railroad shops and offices are still at McCloud although it is no longer a company town as before. Railroad has continuous annual programs for both rail and tie replacement and management is very optimistic about the future.

McCloud River Railroad (Continued)

In 1967 U.S. Plywood-Champion Papers, Inc. purchased 50 new Ramco all-door box cars at a cost of 1½ million dollars. These cars are used to ship forest products from McCloud to customers in all parts of the country. Cars were built by Southern Iron & Equipment Co., Atlanta, Ga.

Correction: P. N. Myers, former McCloud River RR president. Name is incorrectly spelled "Meyers" on pages 72 and 74.

Roster changes and comments:

Steam

#18   Sold to Yreka Western Dec. 1955. This was the "show" engine of the road and when new was on exhibition at the Panama Pacific International Exposition in San Francisco in 1915 (see page 85).

#19   Purchased from United Mining & Smelting Co. of Laredo, Texas in 1923. Possession taken in Mexico City. Sold to Yreka Western in 1953 and is in operating condition.

#23   Sold to Arcata & Mad River Railroad in 1953. Renumbered #11.

#25   Last remaining steam locomotive on the McCloud. Operation condition although requires overhaul.

#26   Sold for scrap through Luria Bros. Co., San Francisco brokers, Nov. 1955.

Diesel Electric

Number	Type	Builder	Serial	Date	Horsepower
28	Diesel-electric	Baldwin	73653	1948	1500
	(Scrapped for parts)				
29	Diesel-electric	Baldwin	74812	1950	1500
	(Sold to Magma Arizona R.R.) 1969				
30	Diesel-electric	Baldwin	75912	1953	1200
	(Sold to Rayonier Corporation 1963)				
31	Diesel-electric	Baldwin	75913	1953	800
	(Sold to Magma Arizona R.R. 1969)				
32	Diesel-electric	Baldwin	76024	1955	1200
	(Sold to Chrome Crankshaft Co. 1969)				
33	Diesel-electric	Baldwin	76105	1955	1200
	(Sold to Chrome Crankshaft Co. 1969)				
34	Diesel-electric	Baldwin	75449	1952	1600
	(Ex-S.P. #5253 — Sold to Oregon & Northwestern R.R. 1969)				
35	Diesel-electric	Baldwin	74261	1949	1600
	(Ex-S.P. #5207 — Sold to U.S. Steel Corp. 1969)				
IN SERVICE:					
36	Diesel-electric	E.M.D.	34880	1969	2000
37	Diesel-electric	E.M.D.	34881	1969	2000
38	Diesel-electric	E.M.D.	34882	1969	2000

LOCOMOTIVES OF THE QUINCY RAILROAD

Number	Type	Builder	Serial	Date	Driv.	Cyl.	Tract. Force	Boil. Pres.	Tot. Wt.
1	0-4-4T	Pitts. (Amer.)	#46915	1909	44	14x20	13630	180	74000

Purchased new. Sold July 1947. Became stationary boiler at a cedar mill near Quincy.

Number	Type	Builder	Serial	Date	Driv.	Cyl.	Tract. Force	Boil. Pres.	Tot. Wt.
2*	2-6-2T	Schen. (Amer.)	#65032	1924	44	16x24	21400	180	119700

Purchased new. Still used as a standby.

Number	Type	Builder	Serial	Date	Driv.	Cyl.	Tract. Force	Boil. Pres.	Tot. Wt.
3*	Diesel-electric-American		......	1945	....	......	380 hp	...	88000

Powered by two Caterpillar V-8 engines. Electrical equipment by General Electric.

*In service.

MISCELLANEOUS EQUIPMENT: Freight cars, 1.

SUPPLEMENTARY INFORMATION – 1971

Quincy Junction to Feather River Lumber Co. near Quincy, Calif. – 3 miles

Full-time employees: four. Three seasonal track laborers during summer.

Previous owner, the Quincy Lumber Company was purchased on Feb. 6, 1956 by the Meadow Valley Lumber Company; stock purchase included the Quincy Railroad. On March 1, 1968 Meadow Valley was purchased by the Feather River Lumber Co., the railroad again included. Legal title is with the DiGiorgio Lumber Co., dba Feather River Lumber Co., a subsidiary of the DiGiorgio Corp. of San Francisco.

Effective Dec. 31, 1969 railroad terminated service into the town of Quincy proper, abandoning 2.2 miles of main line and 0.84 miles of other track, terminating the line at the Feather River Lumber Co. mill where a new engine house, loading dock and office were built. Buildings in town have been abandoned and all of the right-of-way property is being bought by the county. Local freight had fallen to trucks, and since the railroad's main customer is the mill this move was justified.

In 1968 a program of installing heavier rail and more ballast was started. Ballast program was completed summer 1970 and a half mile of #75 rail a year is present replacement schedule.

Roster changes:

The road's remaining steam locomotive #2 was sold in Aug. 1970 to "Iron Horse Railroads, Inc.", a Bay Area rail fan group. All work is now done with Diesel #3.

LOCOMOTIVES OF THE SIERRA RAILROAD

Number	Type	Builder	Serial	Date	Driv.	Cyl.	Tract. Force	Boil. Pres.	Tot. Wt.
1	4-4-0	....	......	.....				...	......

Acquired for construction of road and disposed of after completion. No authentic records.

Number	Type	Builder	Serial	Date	Driv.	Cyl.	Tract. Force	Boil. Pres.	Tot. Wt.
2	4-4-0	....							

First #2 similar to #1. No other information available.

Number	Type	Builder	Serial	Date	Driv.	Cyl.	Tract. Force	Boil. Pres.	Tot. Wt.
2	0-6-0	New York	# 506	1889	44	18x26	25000	155	94500

Built as Montana Union No. 109, Northern Pacific No. 929, to Sierra, resold to Lassen Lumber & Box Co., Susanville, Calif, where it became No. 23 (1918), sold to Red River Lumber Co. (1929), scrapped September, 1940.

Number	Type	Builder	Serial	Date	Driv.	Cyl.	Tract. Force	Boil. Pres.	Tot. Wt.
3	4-6-0	Rogers	# 4493	1891	56	17x24	17470	160	100000

Built as Prescott & Arizona Central No. 3. Brought to the Sierra in 1897. Retired in 1932, but retained for motion picture work.

Number	Type	Builder	Serial	Date	Driv.	Cyl.	Tract. Force	Boil. Pres.	Tot. Wt.
4	4-4-0	Baldwin	# 5851	1882	62	17x24	13790	145	80000

Built as Northern Pacific No. 99. Renumbered NP 652 before coming to Sierra. Sold to Pickering Lumber Co. 1917, renumbered 14, scrapped 1938.

Number	Type	Builder	Serial	Date	Driv.	Cyl.	Tract. Force	Boil. Pres.	Tot. Wt.
5	0-6-0	Schen.	# 5177	1899	..	......		...	......

Sold about 1903 to Hawaii Consolidated RR.

Number	Type	Builder	Serial	Date	Driv.	Cyl.	Tract. Force	Boil. Pres.	Tot. Wt.
6	4-4-0	Baldwin	# 6113	1883	62	17x24	13790	145	80000

Built as Northern Pacific No. 114. Renumbered NP 653 before coming to Sierra. Sold to Atlas-Olympia Co. plant near Oakdale, Calif. Last used as stationary boiler. Scrapped 1937.

LOCOMOTIVES OF THE SIERRA RAILROAD (Cont'd.)

Number	Type	Builder	Serial	Date	Driv.	Cyl.	Tract.Force	Boil.Pres.	Tot. Wt.
7	4-4-0	Baldwin	# 5674	1882	62	17x24	13790	145	80000
	Built as Northern Pacific No. 93. Resold.								
8	No known locomotive of this number.								
9	Heisler	Heisler	# 1036	1899	40	16¾x14	20000	160	104000
	Sold to Pickering Lumber Co. No. 8, West Side Lumber Co. No. 1, scrapped 1947.								
10	Shay	Lima	# 718	1902	36	12x12	21500	180	110000
	Sold to Diamond Match Co., 1917.								
11	Shay	Lima	# 788	1903	36	12x12	21500	180	110000
	Sold Pickering Lumber Co. 1918, Verdi Lumber Co., Clover Valley Lumber Co. Retained same number.								
12	Shay	Lima	# 789	1903	36	14½x12	29100	180	159600
	Sold to Pickering Lumber Co., 1924. Kept same number.								
13 to 17 and odd numbers 19 to 41 were never assigned.									
18	2-8-0	Baldwin	# 29790	1906	42	18x22	26010	180	111850
	Retired 1953.								
20	2-8-0	Baldwin	# 43344	1916	42	18x22	26010	180	118850
	Sold to U.S. Army in 1942, became No. 6814, resold to Kurth Lumber Co., Jasper, Texas. Renumbered No. 20.								

Number	Type	Builder	Serial	Date	Driv.	Cyl.	Tract. Force	Boil. Pres.	Tot. Wt.
22	2-8-0	Baldwin	#53205	1920	42	18x22	26010	180	121000

Sold to Calif. Western, 1940, became No. 41. Scrapped.

24	2-8-0	Baldwin	#39577	1912	50	20x26	35360	200	163000

Built as Nevada Copper Belt No. 3, purchased by Sierra 1921, retired January 1955. Sold to The Purdy Co. of So. San Francisco for scrap Sept. 1955.

26	2-6-0	Baldwin	#32646	1908	48	18x24	24800	180	124000

Built as Ocean Shore No. 6, purchased about 1921, resold Davies-Johnson Lumber Co, Calpine, Calif., about 1924. Scrapped 1939.

28	2-8-0	Baldwin	#55246	1922	48	19x26	30750	185	142000
30	2-6-2	Baldwin	#55412	1922	42	15x24	19130	175	98000

Said to have been built for the Angels Camp branch. Sold in 1937 to the Howard Terminal Ry. of Oakland. Converted to a 2-6-2T.

32	2-6-2	Baldwin	#57010	1923	46	16x24	20440	180	106200

Sold to Tidewater Southern Ry. 1940, later renumbered 132. After accident on Tidewater Southern, acquired tender from Sierra 18. Used as stationary boiler at sulphur mine 58 miles west of Winnemucca, Nevada.

34	2-8-2	Baldwin	#58679	1925	46	19x26	34690	200	175000
36	2-8-2	Schen.	#68278	1930	50	21x28	42000	200	207000
38	2-6-6-2	Baldwin	#61781	1934	51	31-20x28	59600	225	293000

LOCOMOTIVES OF THE SIERRA RAILROAD (CONTINUED)

Number	Type	Builder	Serial	Date	Driv.	Cyl.	Tract. Force	Boil. Pres.	Tot. Wt.
	Built as Weyerhaeuser No. 4, purchased June, 1952. Sold to Rayonier, Inc., Seattle, Washington. Left Oakdale on Sept. 6 for Hoquiam, Washington.								
40	Diesel-elect. Model S-12. Delivered March 14, 1955, via Santa Fe.	Baldwin	#76092	1955	40	......	1200 HP	...	240000
42	Diesel-elect. Model S-12. Delivered March 18, 1955, via Southern Pacific.	Baldwin	#76093	1955	40	......	1200 HP	...	240000

Note: Unless otherwise noted, engines retained numbers when sold.

MISCELLANEOUS EQUIPMENT: Freight cars, 50. Passenger cars, 4.

SUPPLEMENTARY INFORMATION – 1971

Oakdale to Tuolumne, Calif. — 56.13 miles (main line)

Number of employees: 23

Ownership: Provident Securities Co. of San Francisco, et al.

Roster changes and comments:

STEAM

#18 Baldwin 2-8-0 stripped and sold Sept. 1966 to West Coast Trailer Sales lot in Sacramento. In 1952 its tender was sold to the Tidewater Southern to use with their #132.

#28 Still serviceable.

#34 Sold to White Mountain Scenic Railway, Taylor, Arizona.

#36 Sold to White Mountain Scenic Railway, Taylor, Arizona.

LOCOMOTIVES OF THE SIERRA RAILROAD (CONTINUED)

DIESEL ELECTRIC
(in service)

Number	Type	Builder	Serial	Date	Driv.	Cyl.	Tract. Force	Boil. Pres.	Tot. Wt.
#40	BLH Model S-12	Baldwin #76092		1955		40" Whls.	1200 hp		Tot. Wt. 240,000
	Delivered March 14, 1955 via Santa Fe.								
#42	BLH Model S-12	Baldwin #76093		1955		40" Whls.	1200 hp		Tot. Wt. 240,000
	Delivered March 18, 1955 via Southern Pacific.								
#44	B-B Model S-12	Baldwin #75140		1951		40" Whls.	1200 hp		Tot. Wt. 240,000
	Originally Sharon Steel Co. #2, Sharon, Penn. Delivered at Oakdale, Sept. 21, 1966. Rebuilt at the Sierra Shops and put in service Sept. 5, 1967.								

LOCOMOTIVES OF THE NEVADA NORTHERN

Number	Type	Builder	Serial	Date	Driv.	Cyl.	Tract. Force	Boil. Pres.	Tot. Wt.
1	4-4-0	Schen.	# 566	1869	63	16x24	.....	.....	.....
	Ex CP 161, SP 1228.								
2	4-6-0	Schen.	# 1307	1881	57	18x24	16230	140	.....
	Ex SP of Arizona 26, SP 106, 1609, 2045.								
3	4-6-0	Schen.	# 1592	1882	57	18x24	16230	140	.....
	Ex SP of Arizona 73, SP153, 1645, 2078.								
4	Unaccounted.								

LOCOMOTIVES OF THE NEVADA NORTHERN (CONT'D.)

Number.	Type	Builder	Serial	Date	Driv.	Cyl.	Tract. Force	Boil. Pres.	Tot. Wt.
5	See #80.								
6	0-6-0	American							
	Became NCC Co. 6								
7	See #11								
8	See #20								
9	Unaccounted								
10	4-6-0	Dickson (American)	#41240 Built as #4.	1906	56	20x26	25000	180	276000
11	4-6-0	American	#42662	1907	56	20x26	25000	180	276000
	Ex No. 7								
20	4-6-0	Rogers	#37573	1907	58	19x26	26130	190	289000
21	4-6-0	American	......	1909	58	19x26	......	190	289000
40*	4-6-0	Baldwin	#34942	1910	69	19x26	23100	200	274000
80	2-8-0	American	#41327, Ex No. 5.	1906	48	19x26	33240	200	320000
	Formerly a saddle tank, 2-8-2T, Ex No. 5.								
81*	2-8-0	Baldwin	#45351	1917	51	21x26	36200	190	323000
	Equipped with mechanical stoker.								

Note: All of the above were coal-burners. *Nos. 40 and 81 are out of service, but stored at East Ely. The others have been scrapped or otherwise disposed of.

LOCOMOTIVES OF THE NEVADA NORTHERN (CONTINUED)

Number	Type	Builder	Serial	Date	Driv.	Cyl.	Tract. Force	Boil. Pres.	Tot. Wt.
401	Diesel-electric EMD SD-7 Six axles.			1952	. .	. . . . .	1500 hp	. . .	294000

MISCELLANEOUS EQUIPMENT: Freight cars 25, Cabooses 2, Combination car 1, Baggage car 1, Chair car 1, Cadillac inspection car 1, 100 Ton Railway crane 1. Rotary Snow Plow.

KENNECOTT COPPER CORPORATION

Number	Type	Builder	Serial	Date	Driv.	Cyl.	Tract. Force	Boil. Pres.	Tot. Wt.
90	2-8-0	American	#43289	1907	51	21x30	42000	190	335000
91	2-8-0	American	. . . . .	1907	51	21x30	42000	190	335000
92	2-8-0	American	. . . . .	1908	51	21x30	42000	190	335000
93*	2-8-0	American	. . . . .	1909	51	21x30	42000	190	335000
94	2-8-0	American	#46927	1909	51	21x30	42000	190	335000
95	2-8-0	American	. . . . .	1914	51	21x30	42000	190	344000
96	2-8-0	American	. . . . .	1916	51	21x30	42000	190	344000
97	2-8-0	American	. . . . .	191(?)	51	21x30	42000	190	318000
98	2-8-0	American	#67943	1929	51	23x28	47000	190	354000

Note: These coal-burning locomotives were used on the "Ore Line" and ran from the mine at Ruth to the mill at McGill, Nevada, about 22 miles. Diesel-electrics have now completely replaced steam, both in the pit and on the "Ore Line".

*All of the above have been scrapped except #93 which is, at present, stored at East Ely. Class 100 Diesels used on the "Ore Line". Some of the 90-series carried Nevada Northern lettering for a time.

Steam locomotives used in the pit were 85 ton tank engines and were housed and maintained at Ruth.

Not listed, but a part of this operation are a number of ore cars of 75 ton capacity, waste cars of 56 ton capacity and several four wheel cabooses.

The rolling stock is owned by Kennecott and maintained at the Nevada Northern shops at East Ely. Train movements and employes are supervised by Nevada Northern management and operate over N.N. rails by trackage agreement.

No. 80 Electric freight motor, 1937 General Electric, 750 volt. Used at the smelter yard as McGill for spotting cars. About two miles of catenary in this yard.

SUPPLEMENTARY INFORMATION – 1971

Cobre to Ely, Nevada – 140.3 miles (main line)

Number of employees: 110

Operates as a wholly owned subsidiary of the Kennecott Copper Corporation. Maintains freight service between East Ely and Cobre with three trips per week. The bus service to Wells was abandoned in 1968.

Locomotives of The Nevada Northern (Continued)

All rail has been removed from the Pit at Ruth and Kimberly and ore and waste are now handled by 75-ton and 120-ton trucks from the pits. Liberty Pit is no longer being mined and all ore is at present coming from the Veteran Pit at Kimberly.

Equipment: 1 EMD Diesel electric 1500 hp locomotive (see page 187)

1 Steam passenger locomotive (#40) stored unserviceable at East Ely (see page 178)

23 Freight cars

1 Wrecking Crane 100-ton capacity

1 Brownhoist Crane 80-ton capacity

2 Passenger cars (stored serviceable at East Ely)

In 1969 Kennecott Copper Corp. purchased a 1200 hp Baldwin Diesel #75548, a 120-ton switcher to operate in the smelter yards at McGill, Nevada. Built 6/25/52 for the New York Central it was overhauled in the S.P. shops in L.A. and numbered KCC #1, was to be renumbered #802.

The White Pine County Public Museum in Ely has on display steam locomotive #81, formerly used by the Nevada Northern on its freight run to Cobre, and KCC #93 a 2-8-0 formerly used on the ore trains between Copper Flat and the mill.

LOCOMOTIVES OF THE NEVADA COPPER BELT RAILROAD

Number	Type	Builder	Serial	Date	Drive	Cyl.	Tract. Force	Boil. Pres.	Tot. Wt.
1	4-6-0	Baldwin	#12204	1891	..	......	....	.....	......

Originally Los Angeles Terminal #7, SP, LA & SL #51, LV & T #No. 2. Damaged in round house fire at Mason, Nevada in 1916 and was scrapped.

Number	Type	Builder	Serial	Date	Drive	Cyl.	Tract. Force	Boil. Pres.	Tot. Wt.
2	2-8-0	Lima	#1091	1911	50	18x24	26400	200	134550
3	2-8-0	Baldwin	#37577	1912	50	20x26	35360	200	163000

Sold to Sierra Railroad where it became #24.

Number	Type	Builder	Serial	Date	Drive	Cyl.	Tract. Force	Boil. Pres.	Tot. Wt.
4	2-8-0	Baldwin	......			.....	.....	.....	......

A coal-burner purchased in the East. Arrived at Sparks, Nevada to be converted to oil, but was sold for junk. Never ran on the N.C.B.

Number	Type	Builder	Serial	Date	Drive	Cyl.	Tract. Force	Boil. Pres.	Tot. Wt.
5	2-8-0	American(Richmond)	#66302	1925	51	19x26	31300	200	150000

Designed for the N.C.B. as a 2-8-2, but the trailing truck was never installed. Sold to the Virginia & Truckee in 1947.

Number	Type	Builder	Serial	Date	Drive	Cyl.	Tract. Force	Boil. Pres.	Tot. Wt.
6	0-6-0	Fate-Root-Heath	......				...	...	......
6	0-6-0	Plymouth							60000

Gasoline powered. 175 hp LeRoi 6 cylinder engine. Purchased second hand 1945.

MOTOR CARS:

Number	Type	Builder	Serial	Date	Drive	Cyl.	Tract. Force	Boil. Pres.	Tot. Wt.
20		Fairbanks Morse	......			.....	.....	...	...

Chain driven combination passenger and mail car. Destroyed by fire.

Nevada Copper Belt Railroad (Continued)

21	Hall-Scott	#	5	1910	 72000

One of the first Hall-Scott gasoline propelled railway cars. Built in San Francisco. Trucks by Brill. Body by Holman of S.F. Car #3, engine #3, transmission #3. 54 feet long, 150 hp, 32 passengers. Purchased by N.C.B. in 1911. Sold to Bay Area Electric Railroad Association 1947.

22	Hall-Scott	#	13	1914	 80000

Steel combination motor. Purchased from the Salt Lake & Utah RR. Trucks by Hall-Scott. 150 hp, 25 passengers, 60 feet long. Car #18, engine #18, transmission #18. Scrapped 1947.

MISCELLANEOUS EQUIPMENT: Cabooses 3, hopper bottom cars 45*, a large number of center dump gondola ore cars, miscellaneous box cars, flat cars and other ore cars.

*In connection with the above mentioned 45 hopper bottom cars, it is interesting to note that only two ever saw the rails of the N.C.B. These cars were purchased new and were supposedly traded for ties which reportedly were never received. Somehow or other these cars wound up on a railroad in Mexico. The entire transaction is rather vague and no one has been able to determine exactly what took place.

SUPPLEMENTARY INFORMATION – 1971

Wabusca to Ludwig, Nevada – 37.8 miles (main line)

Abandoned March 24, 1970

Even while the Nevada Copper Belt Railway was sweating out its abandonment hearings there were rumors that renewed mining activity was about to begin in the Yerrington area. These rumors had greater validity than most mining district gossip and were based on the fact that the Anaconda Company had leased a large piece of property near Mason. There then followed three years of exploration work which revealed a deposit of some forty million tons of oxide ore with a fifteen million ton body of sulphide ore below that.

However, Anaconda could not firm up their plans at that time and so the NCB, faced with continuing deficits, was forced to shut down.

It wasn't until November, 1951, shortly after the outbreak of hostilities in Korea and in answer to the Government's plea for stepped-up copper production, that Anaconda made the decision to develop the Yerrington mine.

Today the huge open pit at Weed Heights yields about 28,000 tons of ore per day (and about the same amount of waste material) which, when processed, amounts to an annual production of seventy-five million pounds of copper. Mining is done by four 5-yard P & H Electric shovels with haulage to the plant and dumps handled by trucks. About 450 people are employed with the mine operating 3 shifts a day, 7 days a week.

All copper shipments are hauled by truck to the Southern Pacific at Wabuska. Any shipments received by rail are unloaded at Wabuska and trucked to Weed Heights also. The Company does not have any plans at present for rebuilding the line to Wabuska, although there has been some talk of other interests wanting to finance and construct a short line. There has also been a lot of talk in the area of other mines opening. No doubt if one or two other large mines were to be developed more interest would be displayed in a railroad that would once again serve the Mason Valley of Nevada.

REFERENCES

American Guide Series. "Nevada, A Guide to the Silver State," Binfords & Mort, Portland, Oregon, 1940.

Coleman. Charles M. "P. G. & E. of California," McGraw-Hill 1952 ————, "History of Plumas County."

"Illustrated Historical Brochure of Tuolumne County," Progressive Association, Sonora, Calif. 1901.

Kneiss, Gilbert K. "Bonanza Railroads," Stanford University Press 1941.

MacMullen, Jerry and McNairn, Jack. "Ships of the Redwood Coast," Stanford University Press, 1945.

Publications of the

    Ely Chamber of Commerce
    Nevada Bureau of Mines
    Yerington Chamber of Commerce
    Yreka Chamber of Commerce

Records and files of the

    California Public Utilities Commission
    California Western Railroad
    McCloud River Railroad
    McCloud Lumber Company
    Nevada Copper Belt Railroad
    Nevada Northern Railroad
    Nevada Public Service Commission
    Parr-Richmond Terminal Co.
    Quincy Railroad
    Sierra Railroad.
    Yreka Western Railroad

Riesenberg, Jr., Felix. "The Story of San Francisco Harbor," Alfred A. Knopf, 1940

Sabin, Edwin L. 'Building The Pacific Railway," J. B. Lippincott Co., 1919.

"The Official Guide of the Railways." National Railway Publication Co., New York.

"The Pocket List of Railroad Officials." The Railway Equipment and Publication Co., New York, 1955.

"The Western Railroader." Francis A. Guido, publisher. San Mateo. Calif.

————. "Tuolumne County, Calif.", The Union Democrat, Sonora, Calif. 1909.

Walker, Jr., David H. "Tuolumne County, Calif.", Sunset Magazine.

And the files of the

    Democratic Banner, Sonora, Calif.

    Ely Record, Ely, Nevada

    Mason Valley News, Yerington, Nevada

    Plumas Independent, Quincy, Calif.

    Plumas National Bulletin, Quincy, Calif.

    Union Democrat, Sonora, Calif.

ACKNOWLEDGEMENTS

For assistance in compiling and checking information the author is indebted to the following:

CALIFORNIA WESTERN

A. T. Nelson, vice-president and general manager of the California Western Railroad and Navigation Company; Dave Daniels of the San Francisco office of the Union Lumber Company; Claude A. King, former chief dispatcher at Fort Bragg; Fred L. Hanson, former superintendent of transportation; Ed Hendrickson, retired engineer; John Galliani, engineer; Russell Todd, former roundhouse foreman; Mrs. J. C. French and Miss Vera French, wife and daughter of the late J.C. French, former superintendent of the California Western.

YREKA WESTERN

The late A. D. Schader, former owner of the Yreka Western; Herbert F. Baker, president; O. G. Steele, vice-president and chief operating offiicer; D. R. Terrett and the late W. L. Minor, former superintendent of the road; Paul R. Dodge, auditor; Harold Thomas, engineer; George Calkins, fireman; Al Glutsch, conductor; Otis Tyre, brakeamn.

McCLOUD RIVER RAILROAD

P. N. Myers, former president and general manager; Flake Willis, president and general manager of the McCloud River Railroad; C. M. Haines, conductor; William J. Lawrence and the McCloud Lumber Company.

QUINCY RAILROAD

Orville A. Myers, superintendent; L. H. Thayer, former superintendent; Leonard Thayer, his son; the late J. F. Moody, former conductor; the late Ed Lonkey, former brakeman; Solon F. Luzzader, engineer; the staff of the Plumas County Library at Quincy.

SIERRA RAILROAD

W. C. Cheney, vice-president and general manager; J. J. Fowler, trainmaster; Gus Swanson, engineer; Bill McCallum, fireman; Mose Baker, conductor; Arthur Cullen and Louie Antone, brakemen; the late W. J. Tremewan, former master mechanic; Mrs. Ruth Ann Newport, curator of the Tuolumne County Museum; Joe Azevedo, son of John Azevedo, former section boss of the Sierra Railroad. H. E. Lloyd, manager and chief engineer Hetch Hetchy Water Supply, Power and Utilities Engineering Bureau; W. W. Helbush, senior civil engineer; Charles L. Reed, artist. "The Steel Trail to the Mother Lode," Copyright 1953 Automobile Club of Southern California. Al Rose, Jr.

NEVADA NORTHERN

H. J. Beem, retired vice-president and general manager of the Nevada Northern; H. A. Fravel, former superintendent; P. W. Hull, cashier & paymaster; H. M. Peterson, general superintendent; W. R. Armstrong, Jr. superintendent and chief engineer; D. B. Armstrong, chief clerk; O. G. Bates of the Ely National Bank; Mrs. C. A. Norton of the Ely Record; A. Todd Davis and the Kennecott Copper Corporation.

NEVADA COPPER BELT

Fred D. Parr; T. A. Goodrick; John Parr Cox; Fred Parr Cox (all of the Parr-Richmond Terminal Company); Franklin E. Koehler; James O'Connor; Jack Devine; Vernon Peterson; J. H. Thompson; G. M. Ludwick; Charlie Newcombe; L. C. Ellis; Mrs. Alta M. McKay; Rex Ricketts; Ted Bergerson; and C. B. Newcombe, mayor of Yerington.

INDEX